Interactive Bulletin Boards

for Reading and Language Arts Grades 1-4

Elaine Prizzi and Jeanne Hoffman

Fearon Teacher Aids
Carthage, Illinois

Simon & Schuster Supplementary Education Group

MAKEMASTER® Blackline Masters

ISBN-0-8224-6256-7
Library of Congress Catalog Card Number: 83-63176
Printed in the United States of America.

1. 18 17 16 15 14 13 12 11

Contents

Introduction

Interactive Bulletin Boards presents bulletin boards that teach with you. Interactive boards stimulate your students to become involved in the learning tasks you have planned. Use our boards to present a new learning topic or unit, to review a previously taught skill, or to inspire your group to try something new.

Our bulletin boards emphasize reading and language skills, but they are designed to give you complete flexibility and versatility with those skills. You may use the objective presented or choose your own. You may use our board layouts as illustrated or create your own board design based on one of the themes. You may use our specific content suggestions or adjust the material to an appropriate level of difficulty to better meet the instructional needs of your students.

The linemasters, based on six child-appealing themes, will simplify bulletin board construction for you. And, in case the interactive approach is unsuitable for your group, each bulletin board can easily be modified into a display-type board. Refer to the instructions and each bulletin board illustration provided.

In this book:

- *Each section emphasizes a theme.*
- *Each section contains linemasters to help you create bulletin boards that present ingenius and effective displays.*
- *Each section presents five or six interactive bulletin board layouts.*
- *Each bulletin board has a reading/language objective.*
- *Each bulletin board description contains an objective, a list of materials, a procedure, and different activities.*
- *Each bulletin board has several variations or suggestions for adaptation to other skill/content areas.*
- *Each bulletin board has alternative caption suggestions.*

Directions for the Teacher

1. Collect the materials and supplies listed in the next section.
2. Decide on a specific learning objective. (See *Planning Notes*.)
3. Select a theme board. If you wish, you can correlate all the boards in your classroom around one theme.
4. Use the linemasters to make enlarged bulletin board items as needed, following the steps outlined in *Enlargements*.
5. In most cases, sizes are not specified in the directions. The size of each bulletin board item is determined by the size of the bulletin board space available to you. All parts of a bulletin board should be in proportion to each other.
6. Choose and cut the background paper and staple it to the board.
7. Follow the step-by-step directions for completing the board you have chosen.
8. When directed to punch a hole in a bulletin board item, be sure to make the hole large enough to accommodate the head of a pushpin.
9. Thumbtack all bulletin board components in place. Step back from the board to judge its overall effectiveness. Make your adjustments and then staple the items to the board.

PLANNING NOTES

1. *Objectives:* Adapt, change, simplify, or enhance our suggestions to meet your teaching goals. For example, the basic layout of the first bulletin board, "Letter Lift," pages 8–9, can be used to make matches from any content area. The students could match the name of a community helper with his/her public office, an animal with its habitat, a factual question with its answer, a digital time display with its clock face time, and so forth.

2. *Level of difficulty:* Each bulletin board is designed to be adapted to your grade/ability level. Modify our content suggestions to the appropriate level, and use the vocabulary you want your students to master.

3. *Distractors:* We strongly recommend the use of distractors to promote flexible thinking. Distractors are items that do not belong to the solution set. Recognizing an item that does not belong is as instructive as recognizing items that do belong. Include distractors in the bulletin board items whenever possible.

SUPPLIES

Save time and prevent aggravation by keeping all of your bulletin board supplies in one box or plastic tub. Use them only for bulletin board construction!

You will need:
- Tagboard
- Stapler (swing-type)
- Scissors
- Pushpins (as many as 50 or so)
- Hole punch
- Thumbtacks
- Felt-tipped markers
- Meterstick or yardstick
- Rubber cement

Nice to have but not necessary:
- Staple puller
- Staple gun
- T-square
- Chalk
- Precut letters
- Brads

ENLARGEMENTS

Follow these easy steps to produce high-quality art for your bulletin boards:

1. Choose the linemaster you need.

2. Use a copier machine to make a transparency of the linemaster. If you do not have access to a copier, trace the linemaster onto a sheet of acetate with an overhead projector pen.

3. Determine the measurements you desire for the finished enlargement.

4. Cut a piece of butcher paper larger than these measurements. (Use white paper if you plan to color the entire enlargement.)

5. Tape the piece of butcher paper to the chalkboard.

6. Project the transparency onto the paper. Move the projector until the image is the correct size.

7. Use a pencil or a felt-tipped marker to trace the image.

8. Turn off the projector and check the enlargement for any details you may have missed copying.

9. Add the finishing touches to the enlargement. You may:
- Color it with felt-tipped markers, crayons, or chalk.
- Cut pieces of construction paper for detail (eyes, mouths, clothing, etc.), and glue the pieces in place.
- Have your students color the enlargement.

10. Cut out the enlargement.

11. File the transparency for future use.

12. Optional: Laminate or cover the enlargement with clear Con-Tact® vinyl. Then you can use the enlargement for several years.

MAKING CAPTIONS

All of the bulletin board layouts have alternative caption suggestions. Change the caption and the manipulative parts and—presto!—you have a new board.

Save yourself the tedium of measuring. Learn to cut captions freehand. Follow these easy steps.

1. Fold your paper into strips of the letters' height.

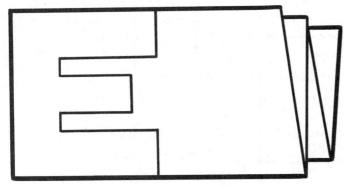

2. Cut through all thicknesses of paper to make one rectangle of the desired width. Use this rectangle as a template for cutting the remainder of the basic letter blocks.

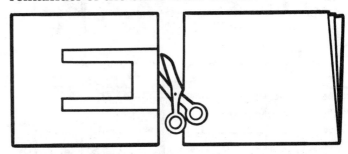

3. Follow the illustration to cut the required letters from the basic letter blocks. Cut a T or an I first to determine the thickness of the letter parts. The dotted lines in the following alphabet show the fold lines for quick cutting.

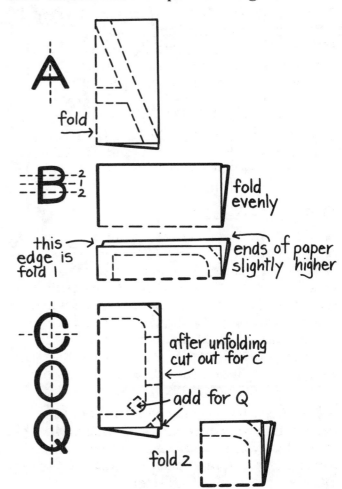

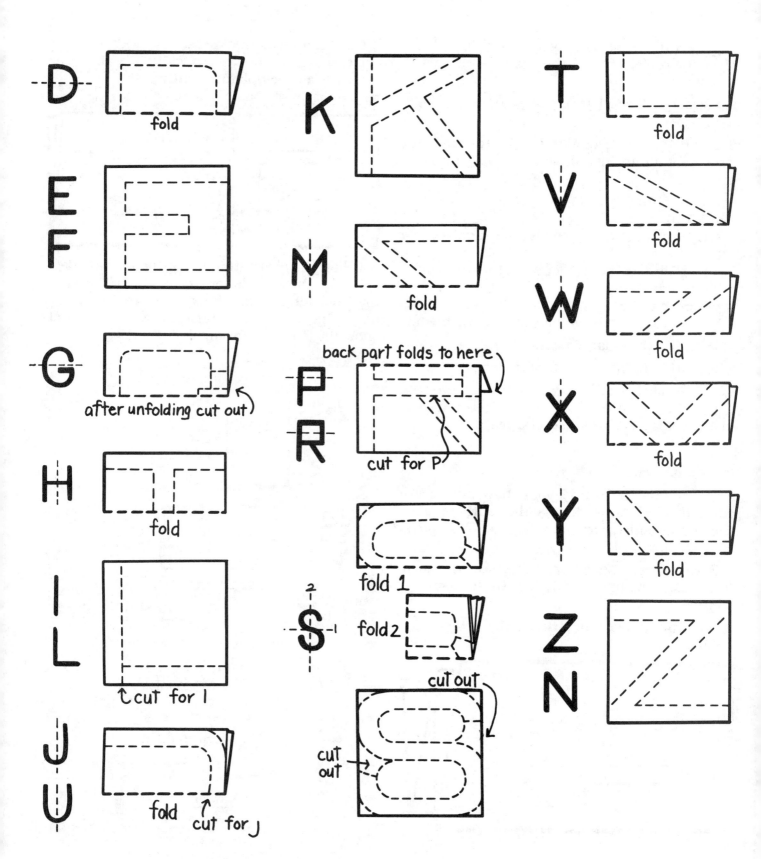

D — fold

E
F

G — after unfolding cut out

H — fold

I
L — cut for I

J
U — fold — cut for J

K

M — fold

back part folds to here
P
R — cut for P

fold 1

S — fold 2

cut out
cut out
S

T — fold

V — fold

W — fold

X — fold

Y — fold

Z
N

4

Other Lettering Styles

Rounded

ABCDEFG
HJKLMNO
PQRSTUV
WXY&Z

Finished

ABCDEFG
HJKLMNO
PQRSTUV
WXY&Z

Square

ABCDEFG
HJKLMNO
PQRSTUV
WXYZ

Super-Quick Caption Techniques

Choose a lettering style—see the suggestions below. Lightly write your caption on construction or other paper. Trace the writing with a felt-tipped marker, and cut out the caption in a block, free-form, or speech balloon shape.

THIS IS A SAMPLE OF BLOCK LETTERING

THIS IS ITALIC LETTERING

THIS IS ALSO A SAMPLE OF BLOCK LETTERING

Lettering Tips

1. The lettering style should be consistent throughout the display.
2. Vertical captions are more difficult to read.
3. Letters should be positioned according to their shapes. Place round letters closer together than straight letters. Irregular letters, such as K, L, and R, should also be placed close together.
4. Balance the spaces between words equally.

Theme 1:

THE CIRCUS

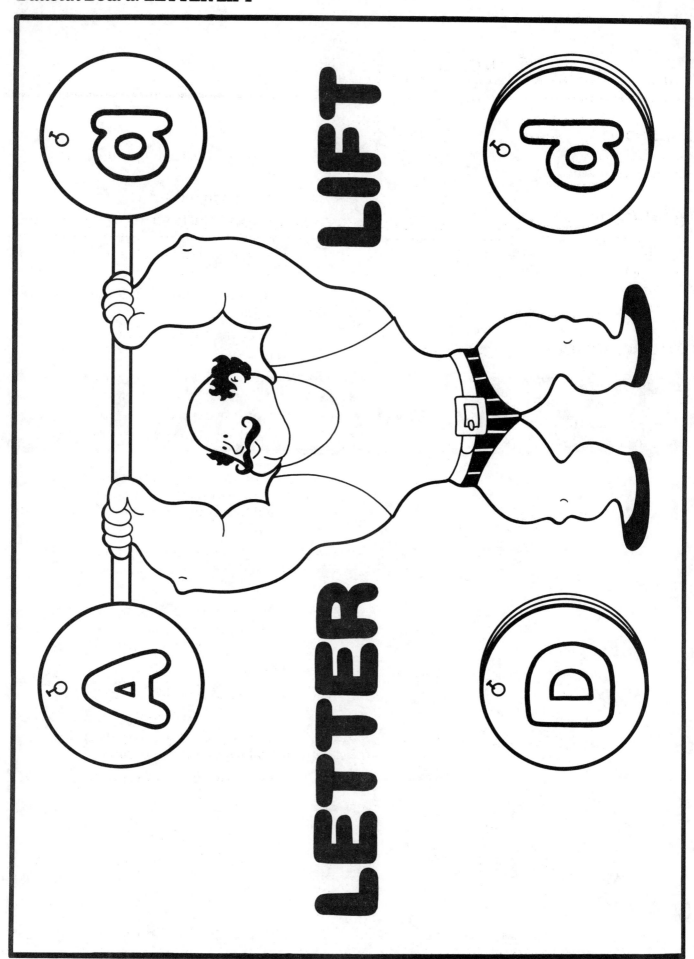

Letter Lift

OBJECTIVE

The students will match upper-case and lowercase letters.

MATERIALS

- Enlargement of the strong man, page 18
- Construction paper for caption
- Tagboard circles
- Four pushpins

OTHER CAPTIONS

- *Be a _____ Lifter* (Place name of skill in blank.)
- *Light Work!*
- *A Not-So-Heavy Load*
- *Balancing Barbells*

PROCEDURE

1. Position and staple the strong man (weight lifter) to the board.
2. Cut out and staple the caption to the board.
3. Prepare two tagboard circles for each letter you wish to present. Print an uppercase letter on one circle and its matching lowercase letter on the second circle. Punch a hole in the top of each circle.
4. Position a pushpin at each end of the bar, a few inches above it, to hold the barbell circles.
5. Position two pushpins near the edge of the board to hold the circles when not in use.

ACTIVITIES

▶ Display all the circles. Suspend one letter circle on the barbell and have the student hang the matching letter circle at the other end of the barbell.

▶ Create a Letter Race. Divide the group into two teams and display all letter circles; after a member from one team suspends a barbell circle, a member from the other team suspends the matching letter circle.

▶ Have the students work independently, matching the displayed letters. Each student is to write the matched pairs on paper.

▶ Have the students match the letters in alphabetical order. Use the entire alphabet or just parts of it.

VARIATIONS

● Print manuscript and cursive letters on the circles for matching.

● Cut out pictures for one set of circles. On the second set, print the letters of the initial sounds for matching.

● Print words with the same terminal sounds on the circles for matching.

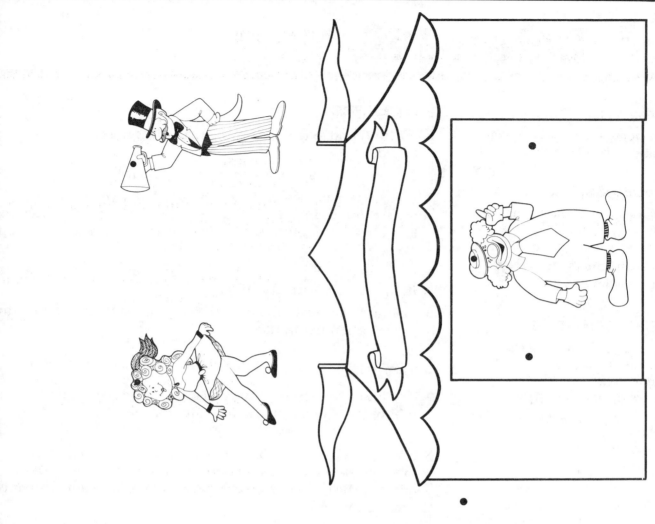

WHERE ARE WE?

1

The clown is in the tent. The ringmaster is above the tent. The ballerina is next to the ringmaster.

2

The ballerina is next to the tent. The ringmaster is next to the tent. The clown is above the tent.

3

The ballerina is above the tent. The ringmaster is in the tent. The clown is next to the ringmaster.

4

The clown is next to the tent. The ballerina is in the tent. The ringmaster is in the tent.

Where Are We?

OBJECTIVE

The students will demonstrate an understanding of position words.

MATERIALS

- Enlargements of the ringmaster, clown, ballerina, and circus tent, pages 19–22
- Construction paper for caption
- 10–15 pushpins
- Set of four paragraphs describing the characters (see example)

OTHER CAPTIONS

- *Hide and Seek, Circus-Style*
- *Up, Down, and All Around the Big Top*
- *A New Parade*
- *I See You!*

PROCEDURE

1. Cut out the caption and staple it to the board.
2. Staple the tent to the board.
3. Position the pushpins around and in the tent.
4. Punch holes in the tops of the figures and suspend them a distance away from the display.
5. Number the paragraphs and staple them to the board.
   Sample Paragraph:
   The clown is in the tent. The ringmaster is above the tent. The ballerina is next to the ringmaster.

ACTIVITIES

▶ Have the students read one of the paragraphs and arrange the figures according to their understanding of that paragraph.

▶ Have the students draw the described arrangements.

VARIATIONS

● Have one student write a story about the characters. Ask a second student to arrange the characters while a third student reads the story orally.

● Staple position words, such as above, in, under, below, right, and left, on the board. Have the students point to them as they are mentioned in a paragraph that is read aloud.

● Make a circus parade using all the characters in this unit. Give different position word commands for the characters and have the students place the characters accordingly.

Catch the Balloons

OBJECTIVE

The students will create compound words from the given word parts.

MATERIALS

- Enlargement of the balloon man, page 23
- 22 tagboard balloons made from the pattern on page 24 (make one larger than the others)
- 22 pushpins

OTHER CAPTIONS

- *Balloon Bonanza*
- *Get Your Balloons Here*
- *Up! Up! and Away!*

PROCEDURE

1. Print the caption on the larger balloon and staple it to the board.
2. Print the directions on the balloon man's balloons and staple the enlargement to the board.
3. Write the compound word parts on the other balloons and punch a hole in the top of each.
4. Position the pushpins randomly on the board and hang the word balloons from them. Draw strings from the balloons if your bulletin board has background paper.

ACTIVITIES

▶ Ask a student to "catch" (choose) a balloon and then list (orally or in writing) as many compound words as he or she can think of for that word part.

▶ Partners or teams may compete to make the most words from a given word part in 30 seconds. The winner takes the word balloon, and the player or team with the most balloons wins. Award real balloons to the winners.

VARIATIONS

● Present compound word parts with exclusive matches using hyphens to indicate whether each is a first or last word part. A set of words to use is mailbox, baseball, earthworm, everybody, horseback, afternoon, headache, spotlight. Ask the students to match the word parts and write the compound words on paper.

● Challenge your students to make the longest string of compound word balloons possible. Line up a row of pushpins on the board. Write a starter word on a balloon and hang it on the first pushpin. To add a balloon to the string, the player must think of a compound word that begins with the last part of the previous word. Example: rowboat, boatman, manhunt. Write the compound words on balloons as they are suggested and hang them on the pushpins.

● Develop variation 2 as a competition for two or more teams. Have the teams compete to see which group can make the longest string within a given time period.

Blendo, the Playful Clown

OBJECTIVE

The students will use the blends **bl, cl,** and **pl** to make words.

MATERIALS

- Enlargement of the clown, page 20
- Tagboard circles of several colors: four large circles, three medium-sized circles, and 25–30 small circles
- Three tagboard rectangles, sized to fit the blend spaces in each small circle
- 30 pushpins

OTHER CAPTIONS

- *Clowning Around*
- *Lots of Dots*
- *In the Ring*
- *Seeing Spots*

PROCEDURE

1. Print the caption on the four large circles and staple them to the board.
2. Staple the clown to the board.
3. Print one blend (**bl, cl,** and **pl**) on each medium-sized circle and staple the circles to the clown as buttons.
4. On the other circles, print the word parts you wish to use with the blends. (Be sure to leave space for the blend rectangle to the left of the word part.) Staple these circles to the clown.
5. Position a pushpin in the blend space of each circle.
6. Print the blend letters on the three rectangular pieces and punch a hole in the top of each.
7. Position a pushpin on the board to hold the blend cards when not in use.

ACTIVITIES

▶ Have the students make words by supplying a blend and pronouncing the words they make.

▶ As an independent activity, have the students write the words. Explain that a word part may be used more than once. Provide a key.

VARIATIONS

● Use only one blend at a time for the activities described above.

● Place only the blend circles on the clown. As the students learn a word that begins with one of the blends, they may write it on a small circle and add it to the board. Use this method for review, too.

● Print sets of word parts that can be used with many blends on the button circles such as **-ank** and **-ing**. Have the students use the blends they have learned to form words. Print the words on the small circles and staple them to the board.

Bulletin Board: RHYME TIME BANDSTAND

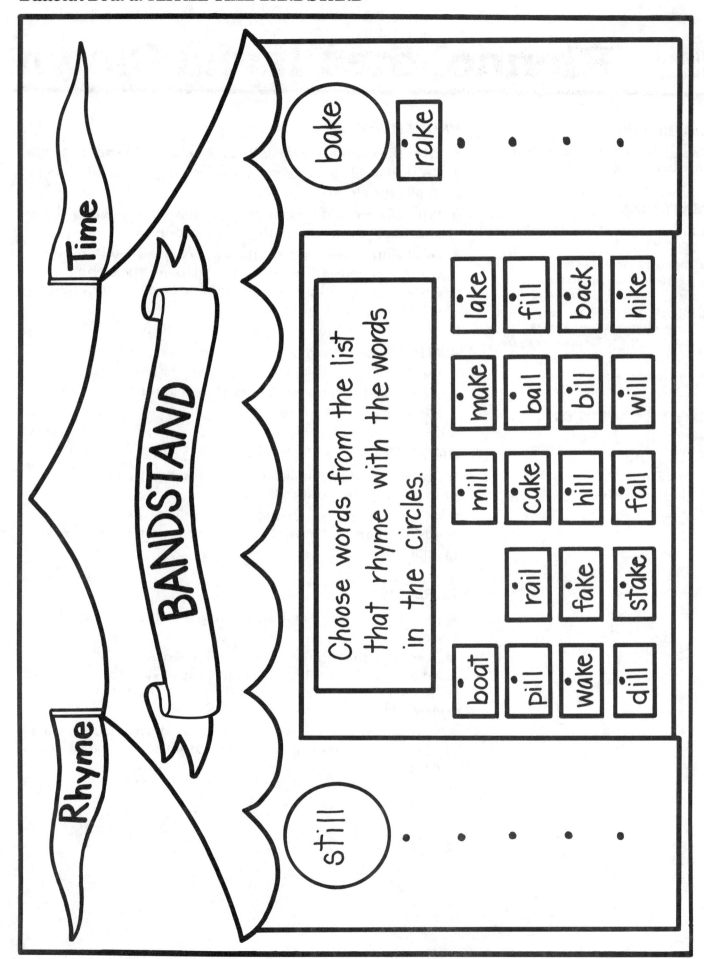

Rhyme Time Bandstand

OBJECTIVE

The students will identify rhyming words.

MATERIALS

- Enlargement of the circus tent, page 22
- Two tagboard circles
- A tagboard rectangle for each word
- Construction paper on which to print the directions
- 30–40 pushpins

OTHER CAPTIONS

- *Under the Big Top*
- *Word Tent*
- *A Slightly Different Tune*

PROCEDURE

1. Print the caption on the tent.
2. On the circles, print the target words for rhyming and staple them to the board.
3. Print the directions on construction paper and staple them to the board.
4. Print the rhyming words on the rectangular cards. Punch a hole in the top of each card.
5. Arrange the pushpins on the board as shown. Hang the word cards on the center pushpins.

ACTIVITIES

▶ Have the students take turns pronouncing a word, then hanging it under the correct rhyming word or discarding it if it doesn't match a target word.

▶ Allow the students to work independently, writing the target words using the list of rhyming words. Provide an answer key.

▶ After the rhyming words are sorted, have the students arrange each list in alphabetical order.

VARIATIONS

● Use picture cards instead of word cards.

● Provide target words on the circles. Have the students write their own rhyming words on the rectangular cards.

● Change the target words and word cards as your students' vocabularies increase.

RINGMASTER

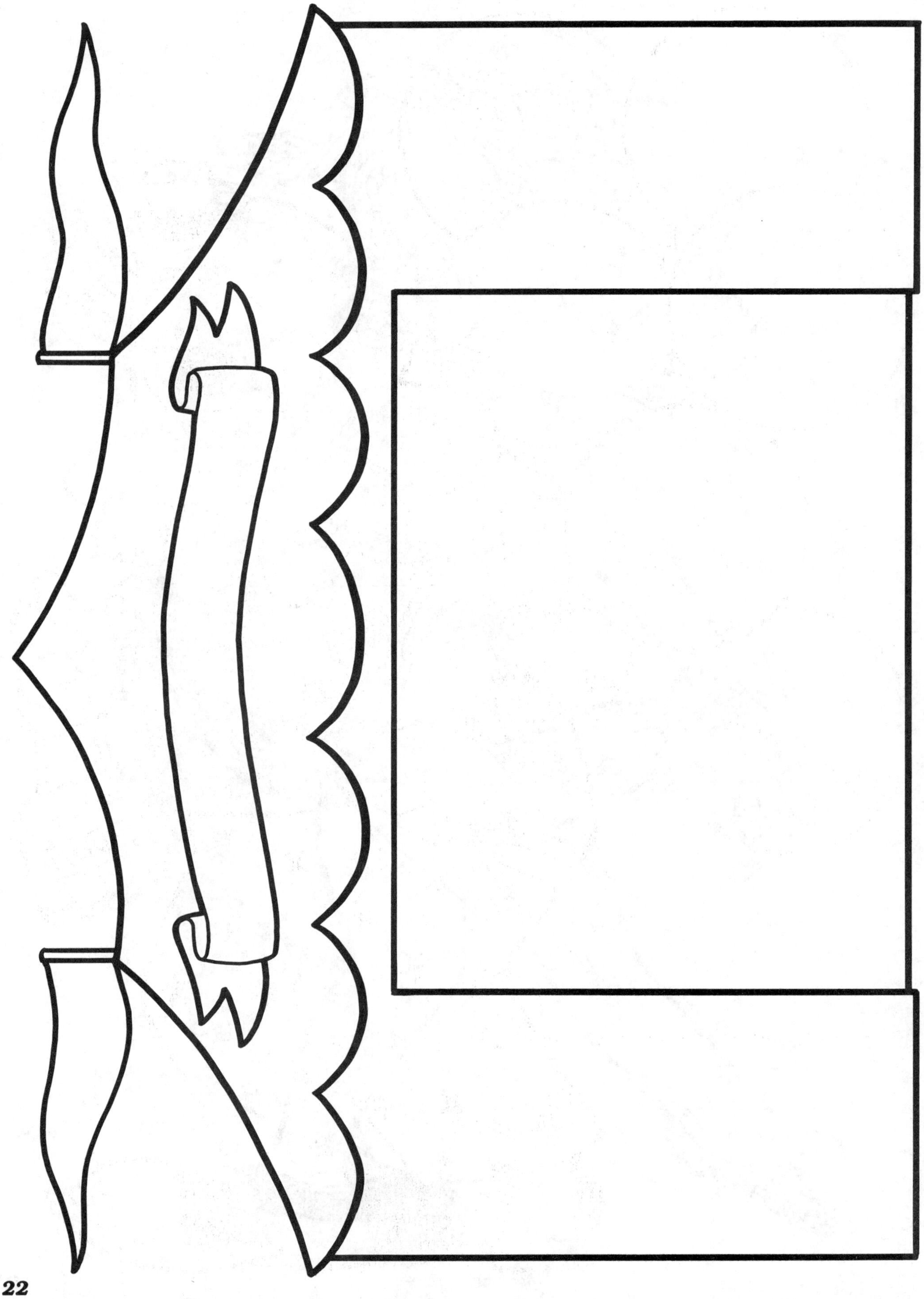

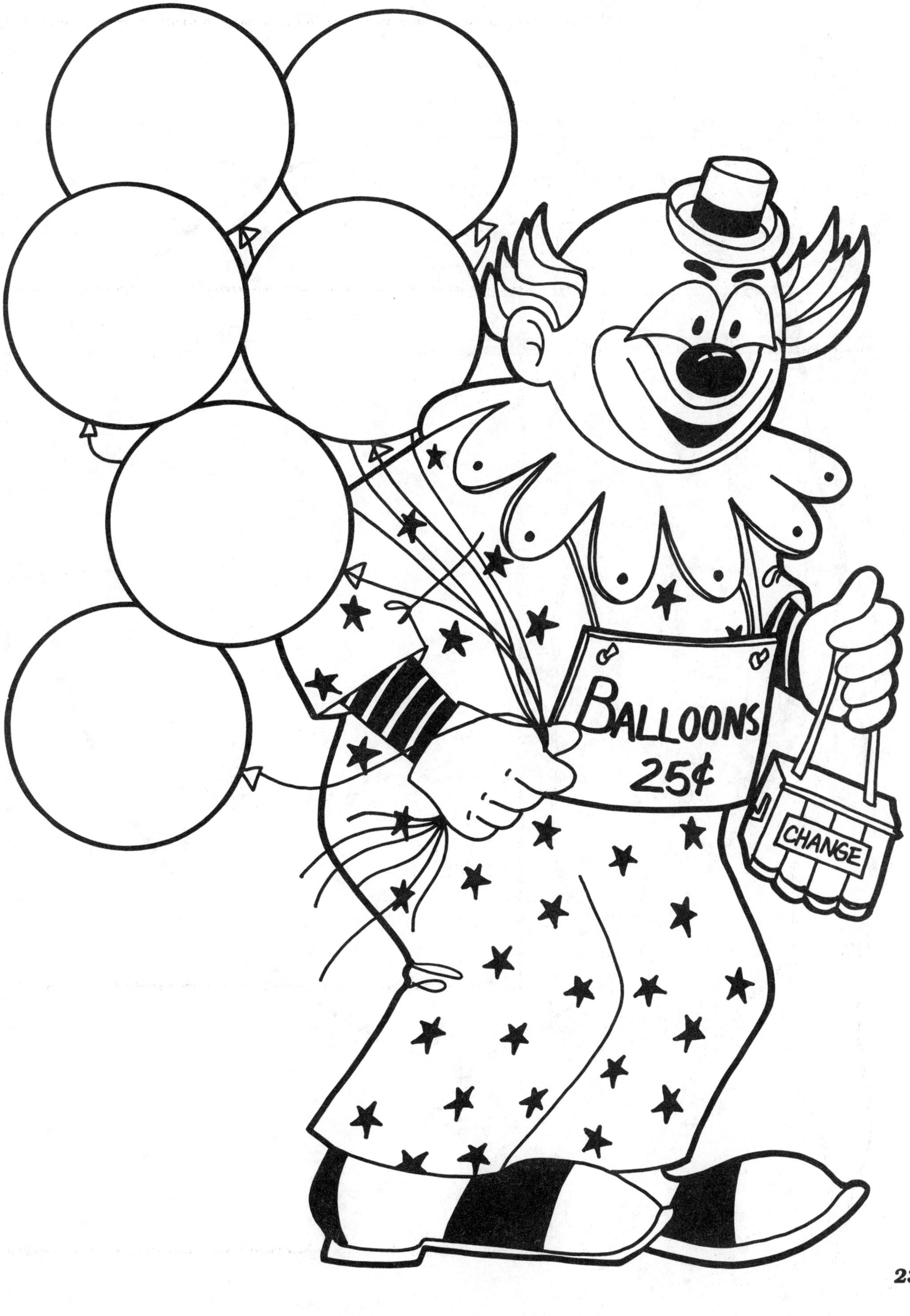
BALLOONS
25¢
CHANGE

BALLOON

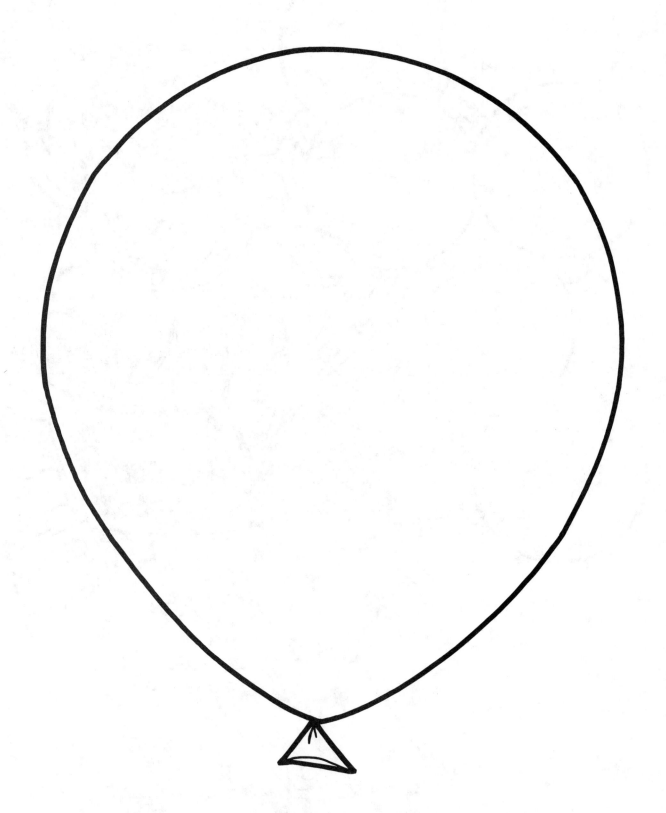

Theme 2:

A Day at the Zoo

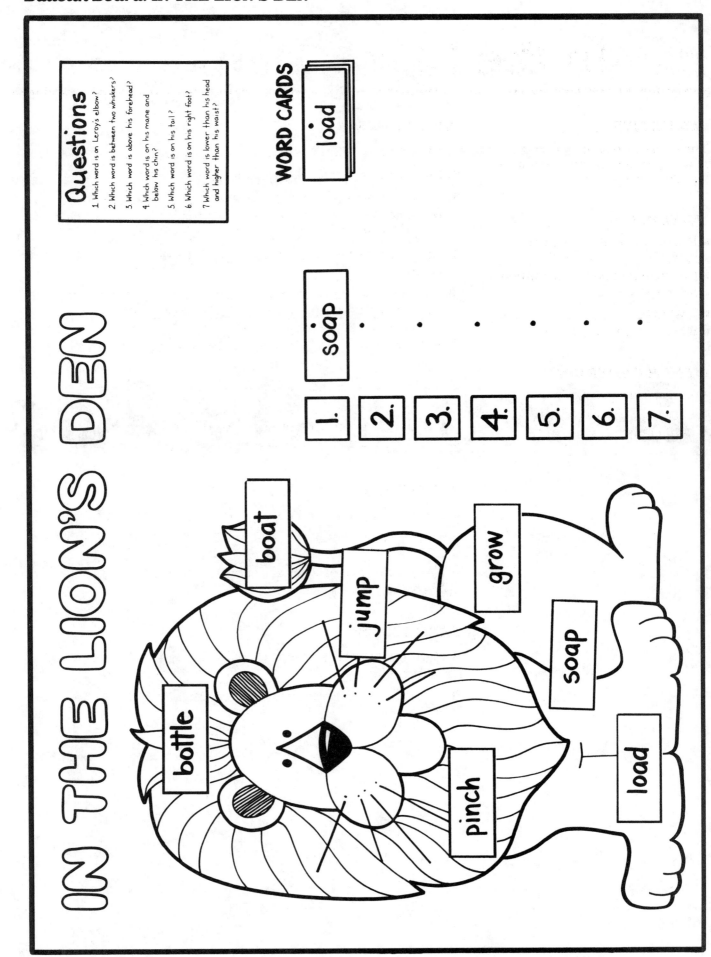

IN THE LION'S DEN

Questions

1 Which word is on Leroy's elbow?
2 Which word is between two whiskers?
3 Which word is above his forehead?
4 Which word is on his mane and below his chin?
5 Which word is on his tail?
6 Which word is on his right foot?
7 Which word is lower than his head and higher than his waist?

WORD CARDS

load

soap

1. 2. 3. 4. 5. 6. 7.

boat

jump

grow

bottle

soap

pinch

load

In the Lion's Den

OBJECTIVE

The students will demonstrate reading comprehension and word recognition.

MATERIALS

- Enlargement of Leroy Lion, page 38
- Construction paper for caption
- Sentence strips
- Tagboard
- 8 or more pushpins

OTHER CAPTIONS

- *Redecorating the Lion's Den*
- *Leroy's Lucky Words*
- *Leroy Says . . .*

PROCEDURE

1. Staple Leroy Lion to the board.
2. Prepare the caption and staple it to the board.
3. Print two sets of seven or more vocabulary words on sentence strips. Cut them apart. Punch a hole in the top of one set of cards.
4. Staple the other set of cards at various places on and around Leroy.
5. On a large piece of tagboard, write a set of questions according to the positions of the cards. For example:
   - Which word is on Leroy's elbow?
   - Which word is lower than his head and higher than his waist?
6. Number the questions and staple them to the board.
7. Make number cards from the tagboard. Staple them to the board and position a pushpin next to each one.
8. Position a pushpin to hold the word cards when not in use.

ACTIVITIES

▶ Have the students take turns reading the questions orally and hanging the correct word cards next to the appropriate number as an answer to that question.

▶ The students can work independently, writing their answers on paper.

VARIATIONS

● Have the students invent their own list of questions using the given display.

● Change the vocabulary words periodically.

Bulletin Board: THE LONG & THE SHORT OF IT

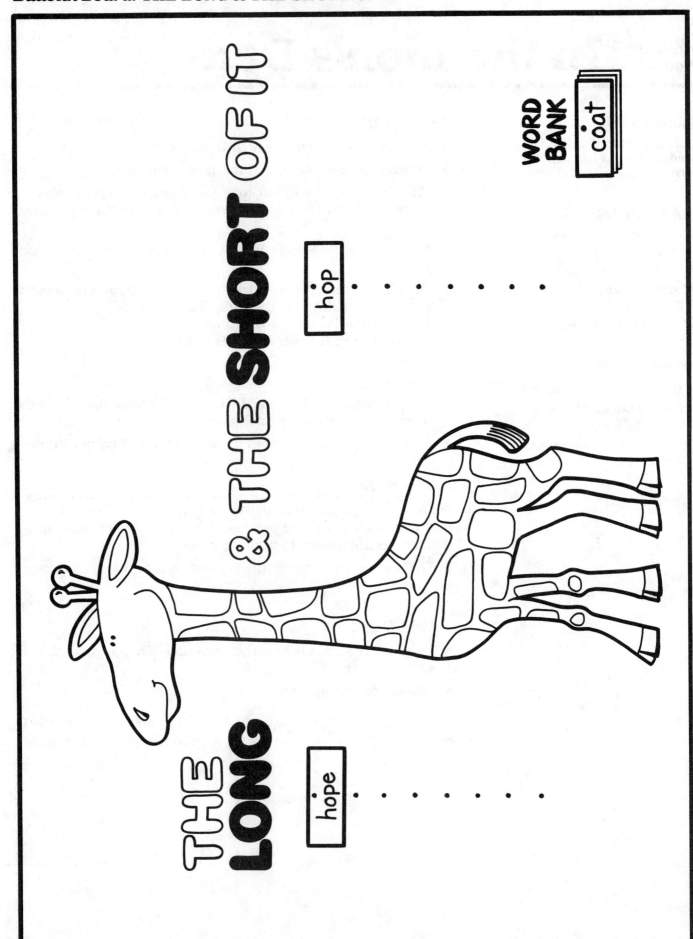

The Long & the Short of It

OBJECTIVE

The students will identify long and short vowel sounds.

MATERIALS

- Enlargement of Jenny Giraffe, page 39
- Construction paper for caption
- Sentence strips or tagboard
- 17 or more pushpins

OTHER CAPTIONS

- *Jenny Jabber*
- *Long on Vowels*
- *Tall Sounds*
- *Short Stuff*

PROCEDURE

1. Staple Jenny Giraffe to the board.
2. Prepare the caption and staple it to the board.
3. Position pushpins under the words **long** and **short** in the caption to accommodate the word cards.
4. Choose eight words with long vowel sounds and eight words with short vowel sounds. Print the words on sentence strips or tagboard. Cut these words apart and punch a hole in the top of each card.
5. Position a pushpin to hold the word cards when not in use.

ACTIVITIES

▶ Have the students sort the word cards according to the vowel sounds and then hang each of them under the appropriate word in the caption.

▶ Have the students work independently to sort the cards and write the words in two columns.

▶ Challenge the students to sort the cards in each category into alphabetical order.

VARIATIONS

● Have the students supply the words to be sorted.

● Subdivide the categories—short a, long e, etc.—as your students' phonics skills develop.

● Provide practice with vowel rules by using subheadings such as double vowel, silent e, single consonant, and double consonant.

● Print word cards with the long and short forms of contractions. Have the students match these pairs.

● To reinforce the meaning of the possessive case, print the long and short forms of possession on sentence strips for matching. Some examples are (1) the hat belonging to Susan, Susan's hat, and (2) the tail belonging to the cat, the cat's tail.

Hide the Honey

OBJECTIVE

The students will identify the ē and ī sounds of a final **y**.

MATERIALS

- Enlargements of Buzzy Bear and Billy Bee, pages 40–41
- Construction paper for the caption, honey jars, pantry, speech balloon, and directions
- 19 or more pushpins

OTHER CAPTIONS

- *A Honey of a Word*
- *Sweet as Honey*
- *Buzzy's Honey*
- *Stocking the Shelves*

PROCEDURE

1. Staple the Buzzy Bear and Billy Bee enlargements to the board.
2. Prepare and staple the caption to the board.
3. Make a speech balloon for Billy and print the caption shown in the illustration. Staple the speech balloon to the board.
4. Cut out honey jars from the construction paper. Print words ending in **y**. Some words to use are rocky, soupy, stormy, salty, curly, windy, handy, reply, deny, try, sky, and cry. Punch a hole in the top of each jar.
5. Position pushpins on the board and suspend the honey jars.
6. Make a pantry by folding a two-inch flap along the long edges of two pieces of construction paper. Staple the folds to the board so that the pieces of paper make doors for the pantry. Print "Pantry" on each door.
7. Open the pantry doors and position pushpins to hold the honey jars.
8. Print these directions on a piece of construction paper and staple it to the board:
   If the word on the honey jar makes an ending sound like the **y** in honey, hide the word in the pantry.

ACTIVITIES

▶ Have the students read the words orally and place the correct ones in the pantry.

▶ Have the students work independently to sort the words. Answers may be written and checked against an answer key.

VARIATIONS

● Have the students supply the words for the jars.

● Have the students arrange the sorted words in alphabetical order.

● Have the students sort the words by the number of syllables.

● On the honey jars, print words that use the two rules for pluralizing words ending in **y**. Have the students sort the words by the rules.

Who Said That?

OBJECTIVE

The students will demonstrate reading comprehension and ability to draw conclusions.

MATERIALS

- Enlargements of all *Day at the Zoo* characters (except the bee), pages 38–40 and 42–44
- Construction paper for speech balloons
- Tagboard
- 7 or more pushpins

OTHER CAPTIONS

- *We Said That They Said . . .*
- *How Did They Say It?*
- *Animals Sounds*
- *Don't All Talk at Once*

PROCEDURE

1. Staple the enlargements to the board.
2. Cut out six speech balloons and staple one next to each character.
3. Print the caption in the parrot's balloon.
4. On tagboard, print a statement about each of the other characters. Examples: "I am the largest of all land animals," or "Honey is my favorite snack." Punch a hole at the top of each tagboard statement. Position a pushpin in each speech balloon for suspending the statements.
5. Position a pushpin on the board to store the statements when not in use.

ACTIVITIES

▶ Have the students read the statements and place each one in the speech balloon beside the appropriate animal.

▶ Display the statements. Have the students work independently, recording the matches on paper.

VARIATIONS

● Have the students write statements for the animals, display them in the speech balloons, and practice reading aloud.

● Prepare statements for the speech balloons that imply different tones or emotions. Statements could be made "happily," "sadly," "angrily," "softly," etc. Make cards for the tone words. Have the students match the tones with the statements.

● Prepare statements for the speech balloons that tell a story if placed in the correct order. Have the students place the statements in order by telling which animal should speak first, second, and so on. A motivational opening might be, "The animals wanted to tell a story, but they all spoke at once. In what order should they speak for their sentences to make a good story?"

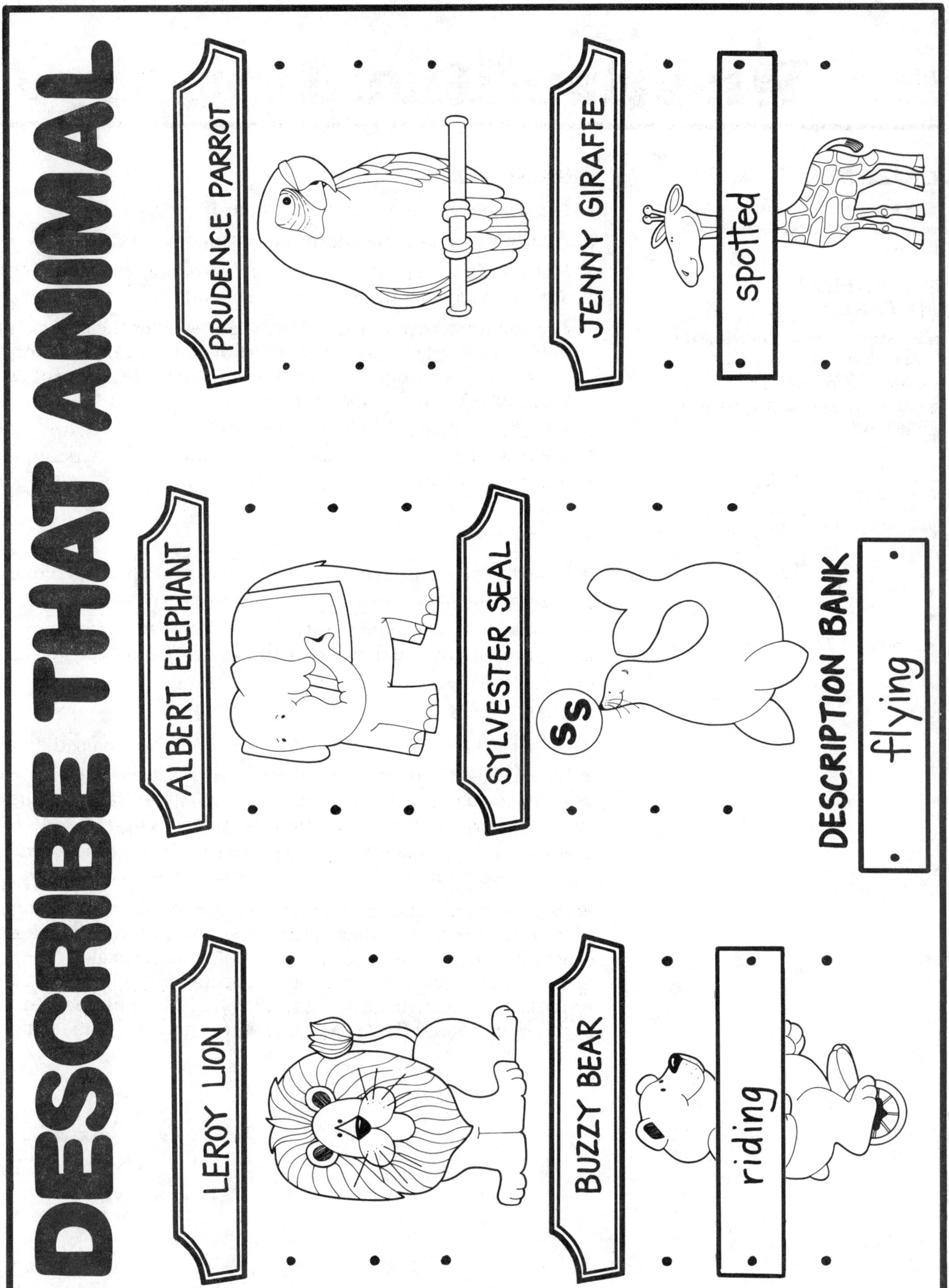

DESCRIBE THAT ANIMAL

PRUDENCE PARROT

JENNY GIRAFFE

spotted

ALBERT ELEPHANT

SYLVESTER SEAL

Ss

DESCRIPTION BANK

flying

LEROY LION

BUZZY BEAR

riding

Describe That Animal

OBJECTIVE

The students will identify animals by their descriptions.

MATERIALS

- Enlargements of the animal characters, pages 38–40 and 42–44
- Construction paper
- Sentence strips or tagboard
- 38 or more pushpins

OTHER CAPTIONS

- *Guess That Animal*
- *The Sound of the Scene*
- *Zoo Keeper's Delight*

PROCEDURE

1. Prepare the caption and staple it to the board.
2. Position and staple the animals to the board.
3. Make a name tag for each animal. Staple each tag above the appropriate animal.
4. Cut the sentence strips to fit across each animal. Punch two holes, one at each end of the strips. Print words on the strips to describe the animals. Examples: fierce (lion); huge, gray (elephant); swimmer (seal).
5. Align the pushpins on the board as shown to accommodate the description strips.
6. Position pushpins to hold the strips when they are not in use.

ACTIVITIES

▶ Have the students read the words on the strips and place them over the appropriate animals.

▶ After the words are in place, have the students use the displayed words in sentences about the animals.

VARIATIONS

● Have the students write their own descriptive words for the animals and print them on the strips. Have the students use their words to compose sentences about the animals.

● Have the students arrange each group of strips in alphabetical order.

● Reinforce an initial, medial, or final consonant sound by having the students contribute words that contain a given sound and also describe the animals.

● To remove the strips, have the students provide synonyms or antonyms for the descriptive words. When a correct synonym or antonym is given, remove the strip.

Sylvester Seal's Syllables

OBJECTIVE

The students will determine the number of syllables in the given words.

MATERIALS

- Enlargement of Sylvester Seal, page 44
- Construction paper for caption
- Tagboard circles: six large, numerous small
- 20 pushpins

OTHER CAPTIONS

- *Balancing Sounds*
- *Bouncing Balls*
- *Alphabet by Sylvester*
- *On the Ball*

PROCEDURE

1. Prepare and staple the caption to the board.
2. Staple Sylvester Seal to the board.
3. In one large circle, print "One Syllable." Overlap two large circles and write "Two Syllables" on the top one. Overlap the three remaining large circles and write "Three Syllables" on the top one. Staple the circles to the board as shown.
4. Print words of one, two, and three syllables on the small circles. Punch a hole in the top of each word circle.
5. Position a group of pushpins under each syllable choice.
6. Position pushpins to hold the word circles when not in use.

ACTIVITIES

▶ Have the students read and sort the words into the correct groups.

▶ After the words are sorted, have the students write the two- and three-syllable words, showing the syllabications. Make an answer key.

VARIATIONS

● Use the basic design to have the students practice sorting words containing a given sound in an initial, medial, or terminal position. For example, if **m** is the sound, place a picture of a mouse in the first big circle, a lemon in the second, and a plum in the third. Glue pictures of items with the **m** sound in different positions on the smaller circles for matching.

● Choose three root words. Print them on the larger circles. Have the students contribute words made from these roots. Write the derived forms on the smaller circles for displaying.

● Divide the alphabet into three sections by printing A–H, I–P, and Q–Z on the larger circles. Print individual letters of the alphabet on the smaller circles for sorting into the correct alphabet section.

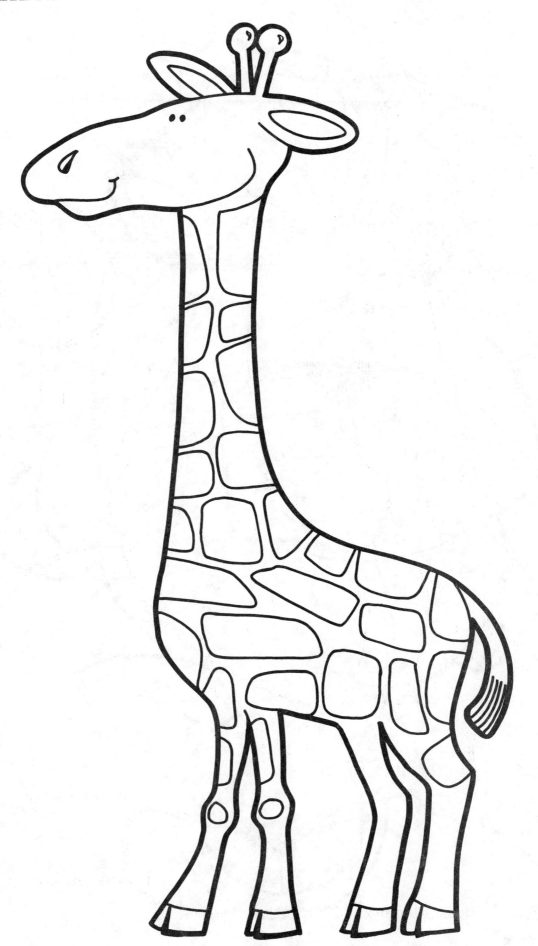

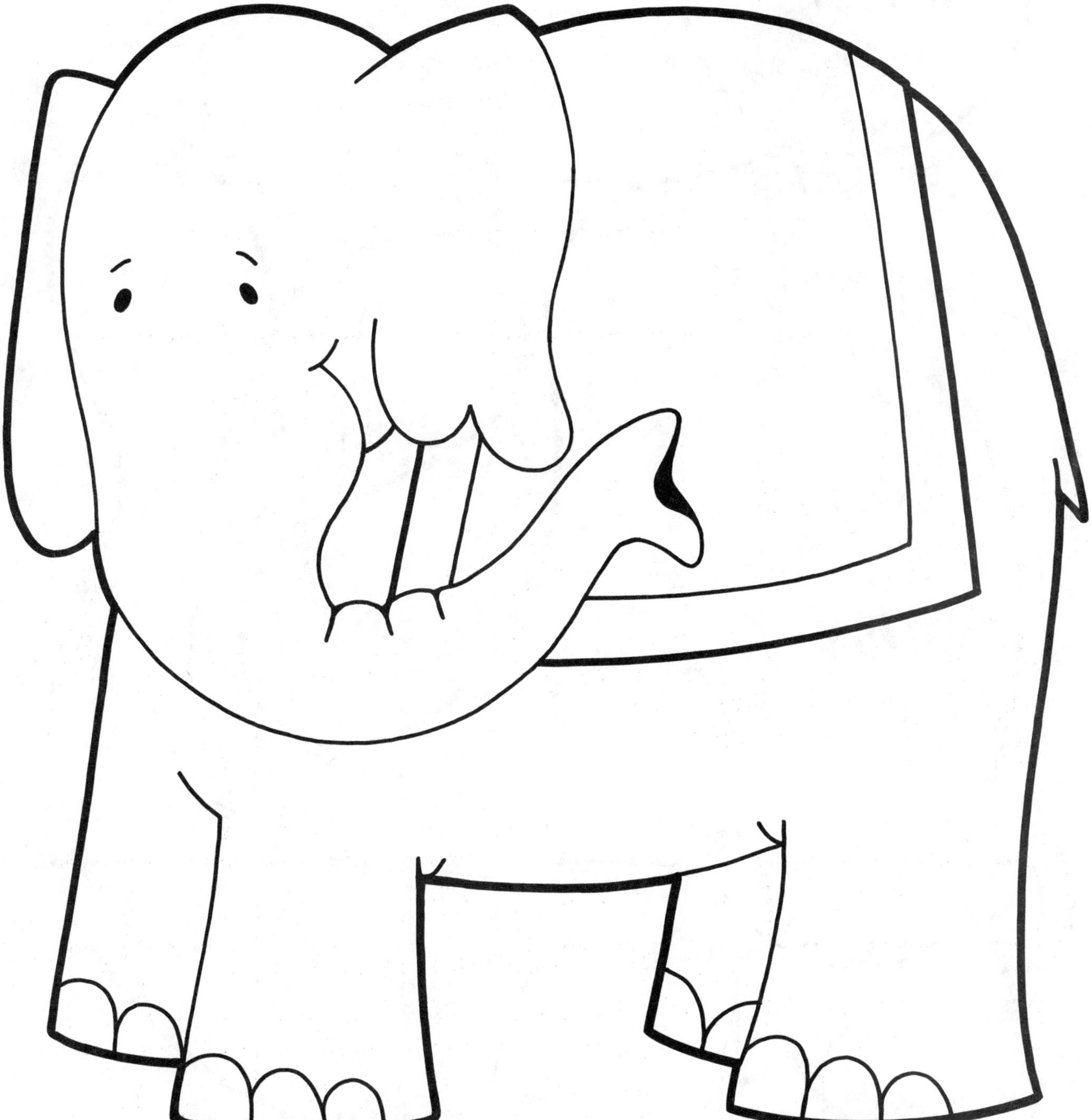

Theme 3:

Around the World

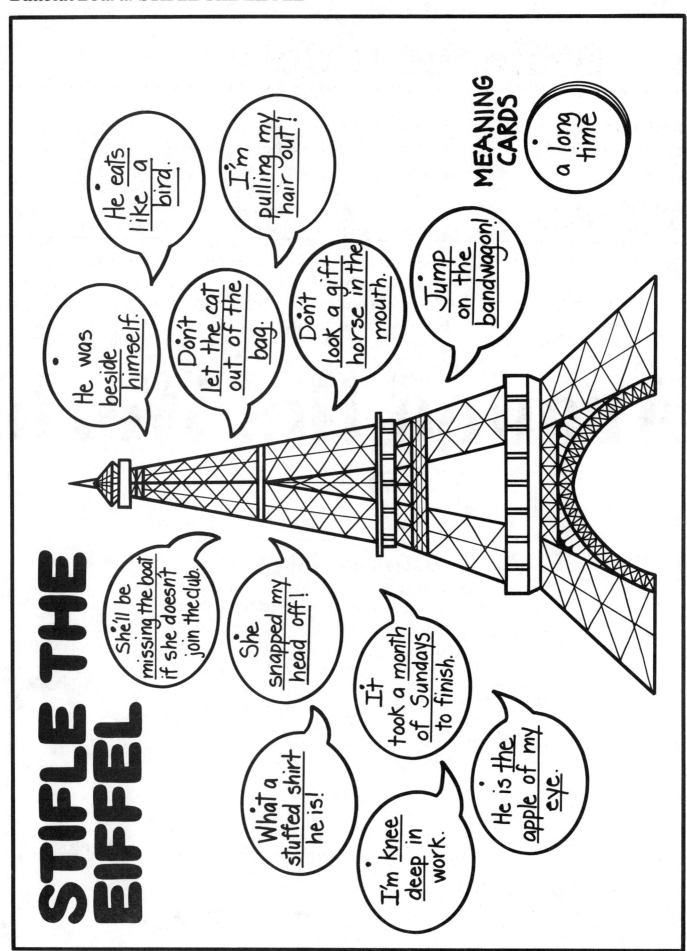

Stifle the Eiffel

OBJECTIVE

The students will interpret idioms.

MATERIALS

- Enlargement of the Eiffel Tower, page 58
- Construction paper for caption
- Tagboard
- 13 or more pushpins

OTHER CAPTIONS

- *It's "French" to Me!*
- *Picture These!*
- *Speak Your Mind*
- *You Don't Say!*

PROCEDURE

1. Staple the Eiffel Tower to the board.
2. Prepare the caption and staple it to the board.
3. Cut out about 12 speech balloons and print sentences on them that contain idiomatic expressions. Use sentences and expressions such as the ones shown in the illustration. Avoid using expressions that have similar meanings. Underline the idiomatic expression within each sentence.
4. Staple the speech balloons around the tower as shown. Put a pushpin near the top of each balloon.
5. Cut out a circle for each speech balloon you make. On the circles, print the meanings for the speech balloon expressions. Punch a hole at the top of each circle.
6. Position a pushpin to hold the meaning circles.

ACTIVITIES

▶ Have the students "stifle the Eiffel" by covering each expression with the circle containing the correct meaning. Discuss the students' choices.

▶ Use the board to display idioms. Have the students supply their own meanings without using the meaning circles.

VARIATIONS

● Have the students illustrate the literal meanings of the idioms and display them next to the appropriate speech balloons.

● Have the students supply other idioms for interpretation.

● Display idioms that deal with a single topic such as speed—"slow as molasses," "quick as a wink," and "as fast as lightning."

THREE COINS IN A FOUNTAIN

Which group of words tells about cats?

1. chase cats

2. usually live in houses

3. speak only in meows

4. play baseball

5. were puppies once

6. eat dog food

7. can climb trees

8. help people learn

9. chase mice

10. read books

QUESTION BANK

Which group of words tells about teachers?

Three Coins in a Fountain

OBJECTIVE

The students will interpret the given facts.

MATERIALS

- Enlargement of the Italian fountain, page 59
- Construction paper for caption
- Sentence strips
- Yellow poster board
- 15 or more pushpins

OTHER CAPTIONS

- *Make a Wish*
- *Coin Toss*
- *Match-Making*

PROCEDURE

1. Prepare and staple the caption to the board.
2. Staple the fountain to the board.
3. Print four questions on separate sentence strips. Suspend one above the fountain and the others in a question bank.
4. On other sentence strips, print several different facts relevant to the questions. Number each fact and staple the strips to the board. NOTE: The facts serve as answers to the four questions. Each question should have about three matching facts, and some facts can answer more than one question. The four questions to use with the facts shown in the illustration are "Which group of words tells about cats?" "Which group of words tells about dogs?" "Which group of words tells about teachers?" "Which group of words tells about children?"
5. Cut small circles from the yellow poster board. These should resemble coins. Number the coins to match the facts. Punch a hole in the top of each coin.
6. Place a pushpin to the left of each fact strip and hang the matching coins on the pushpins.
7. Position three pushpins in the fountain.

ACTIVITIES

▶ Have the students read the displayed question and facts, and then show the correct answers by placing the appropriate coins in the fountain.

▶ Place any three coins in the fountain. Have the students decide if they are the correct answers.

VARIATIONS

● Change the questions and answers.

● Supply facts and distractors and have the students think of the question.

● Give the students a question and have them supply the possible answers.

● Display a statement at the top of the fountain. Print other statements for matching. Some should have the same meaning and some should not have the same meaning as the displayed statement.

MANY STORIES

1. Did dragons really exist? Dragons appear in myths and legends through much of the world. They are almost always pictured as snakes or huge lizards and even sometimes as dinosaurs.

2. In China, dragons were supposed to have been powerful but good. In fact, they were so important that the dragon became a national symbol. In Japan, dragons were supposed to have the power to change their size. Both Chinese and Japanese dragons usually are pictured without wings.

3. The English also believed in dragons. In England, dragons were considered evil. They were so terrible that they became symbols of war. Although dragons are important in many cultures, they were never real creatures.

Dragons did not really exist.	Dragons usually look like snakes.
Dragons are national symbols of China.	Dragons are legendary.
Sometimes dragons are evil.	Dragons look like dinosaurs.
Japanese dragons are able to change size.	Chinese dragons have no wings.

Dragons are symbols of war.

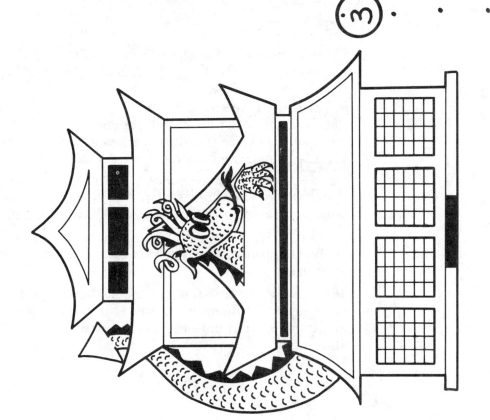

CARD BANK (1) (2) (3)

Many Stories

OBJECTIVE

The students will locate facts to prove the given statements.

MATERIALS

- Enlargement of the Chinese pagoda, page 60
- Construction paper for speech balloons and caption
- Sentence strips
- Tagboard
- 12 pushpins

OTHER CAPTIONS

- *Dragons in Disguise*
- *Interviewing a Dragon*
- *The Dragon Says . . .*
- *Unfinished Stories*

PROCEDURE

1. Staple the pagoda to the board.
2. Prepare the caption and staple it to the board.
3. Choose a topic from social studies or one of general interest such as dragons. Make three speech balloons. In each one, print a paragraph about the topic. See the illustration for sample paragraphs. Number the balloons and staple them to the board.
4. On sentence strips, print separate statements (three per paragraph) based on the information given in the paragraphs. Staple them to the board.
5. Position a pushpin to the left of each statement.
6. Cut nine circles from the tagboard. Number the circles: make three 1's, three 2's, and three 3's. Punch a hole in the top of each circle.
7. Position three pushpins to hold the number circles when not in use.

ACTIVITIES

▶ Have the students read the paragraphs and the statements. Ask them to find the paragraph that proves each statement and to hang a circle with the number of that paragraph beside the statement.

▶ Have the students write the number of the paragraph and the particular sentence that proves each statement.

VARIATIONS

● Have the students write the paragraphs and statements for displaying on the board.

● List facts about a current topic of study in each speech balloon. Have the students write a paragraph or story using the information. Display the completed compositions on the board.

● In each speech balloon, print a story without an ending. Write the ending for each story on the sentence strips.

Touring the Turrets

OBJECTIVE

The students will demonstrate their ability to follow directions.

MATERIALS

- Enlargement of the English castle, page 61
- Construction paper for caption
- Tagboard

OTHER CAPTIONS

- *Windows to Words*
- *Climbing the Turrets*
- *Lords and Ladies of the Castle*

PROCEDURE

1. Prepare and staple the caption to the board.

2. Slit the right, left, and bottom edges of each window and fold the paper up to make flaps. Staple the castle to the board. Number the windows as shown.

3. Cut pieces of tagboard that match the size of each window. Print one direction on each piece of tagboard. The directions, followed correctly, will give a message. Sample directions: 1. Draw seven squares in a row.   2. Begin with the left square and write the numbers **1** through **7** under the squares.   3. In square number 2 and in square number 7, write the letter **e**.   4. In square number 5, write the letter **o**.   5. Write the letter **c** in square number 4.   6. Write the letter **l** in square number 3.   7. In square number 6, write the letter **m**.   8. In square number 1, write the letter **w**.   9. Write your name on your paper and give it to your teacher.

4. Staple the direction cards behind the windows in the correct order.

ACTIVITIES

▶ Direct the students to open the windows in numerical order and follow the directions.

▶ Have one student read the directions aloud while a group of students follows them.

VARIATIONS

● Have the students supply the directions.

● Print behind the first window: "Read all the directions before you begin." The last direction should read: "Now follow only those directions behind windows 2, 7, and 8." Behind windows 3, 4, 5, and 6, print directions such as: "Write the alphabet backwards," or "Count from 100 to 200 by tens."

● Use the windows to post the classroom responsibilities. Write a job behind each window. Make a name card for each student. Punch a hole in the top of each card. Suspend name cards from pushpins on or beside the windows.

PYRAMID POWER

quiet

If you don't talk you are ___ .

The rabbit was ___ across the yard.

The boy drew a ___ .

He was ___ tired after he walked 25 miles.

He poured water from the ___ .

Jane walked ___ the room.

She is ___ to win the prize.

Edward ___ about becoming an actor.

The box is big, ___ not heavy.

These ___ belong on the shelf.

WORD BANK

thinks

Pyramid Power

OBJECTIVE

The students will distinguish words of similar spellings.

MATERIALS

- Enlargements of the Egyptian pyramid and palm tree, pages 62–63
- Construction paper for caption
- Sentence strips
- Tagboard
- 10–15 pushpins

OTHER CAPTIONS

- *Pyramiding*
- *Pyramid Clues*
- *Up and Down the Pyramid*

PROCEDURE

1. Staple the pyramid and palm tree to the board.
2. Prepare and staple the caption to the board.
3. On the sentence strips, print sentences with the target words missing. See the illustration for sample sentences using the following words of similar spellings: quiet and quite, picture and pitcher, hoping and hopping, through and though, thinks and things. Staple the strips to the board in random order. Place a pushpin next to each sentence strip.
4. Cut a tagboard triangle (pyramid) for each target word. Print the target words on the pyramids. Punch a hole in the top of each pyramid.
5. Position a pushpin on the board to hold the pyramid word cards when not in use.

ACTIVITIES

▶ Have the students read the sentences, select the correct word for each sentence, and hang each pyramid word card next to its sentence.

▶ Have the students write the completed sentences on paper.

VARIATIONS

● Display completed sentences with target words underlined. Have the students use the target words in their own sentences using the given sentences as models.

● Print sentences containing words you wish to introduce to the group. Underline the target words. The context of each sentence should enable the students to determine the meaning of each target word. Print the meanings on pyramid cards for matching.

● Print sentences using homographs. Examples:

Lead is a metal.   The wind blew.
Lead the parade.   He will wind his watch.

Print the phonetic spellings on the pyramid cards for matching.

● Print sentences whose meanings become the opposite when just one word is changed. Examples: Please **lock/unlock** the door. **Open/shut** the window. On the pyramid cards, print the matching words that change the meanings.

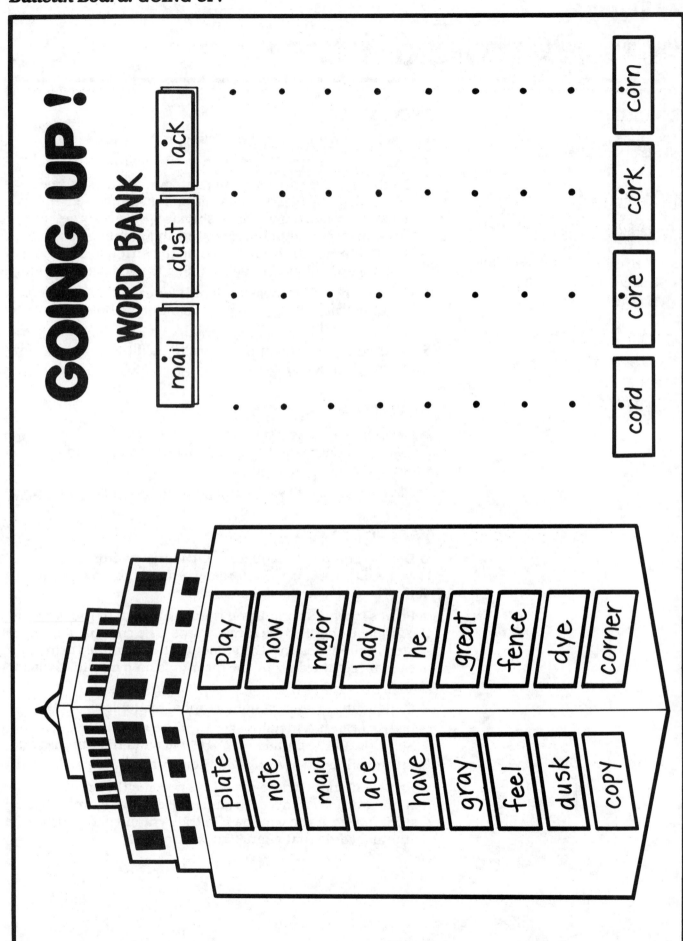

GOING UP!

WORD BANK

mail dust lack

cord core cork corn

plate play
note now
maid major
lace lady
have he
gray great
feel fence
dusk dye
copy corner

Going Up!

OBJECTIVE

The students will be able to use guide words.

MATERIALS

- Enlargement of the Manhattan skyscraper, page 64
- Construction paper for caption
- Tagboard
- 40 pushpins

OTHER CAPTIONS

- *Your Name Please*
- *How Are We Alike?*
- *Skyscraper City*

PROCEDURE

1. Staple the skyscraper to the board.

2. Prepare the caption and staple it to the board.

3. Cut 54 tagboard cards the size of the skyscraper windows.

4. Choose nine pairs of dictionary guide words. Print each guide word on a card. Staple the guide words on the windows in pairs as shown.

5. On the remaining cards, print the words for matching. Make four word cards for each guide word pair. Punch a hole in the top of each card.

6. Position pushpins in horizontal rows beside each guide word as shown.

7. Position several pushpins to hold the word cards when not in use.

ACTIVITIES

▶ Have the students sort the cards and hang them from the pins next to the correct guide words.

▶ Have the students arrange each row of words in alphabetical order.

VARIATIONS

● Use names from the telephone book as guide words, and print names on the cards to be sorted.

● Staple pictures of things that are alike in some way in the adjacent windows. Position two pushpins in each horizontal row. On the cards, print the ways in which the items are alike. Some likenesses could be size, color, shape, or use.

● Display several skyscrapers and give each one a name, such as The Ew Building, The Oy Building, or The Au Building, corresponding to consonant blends or diphthongs. As the students encounter words with these sounds, have them print cards for the words and place them in the appropriate windows.

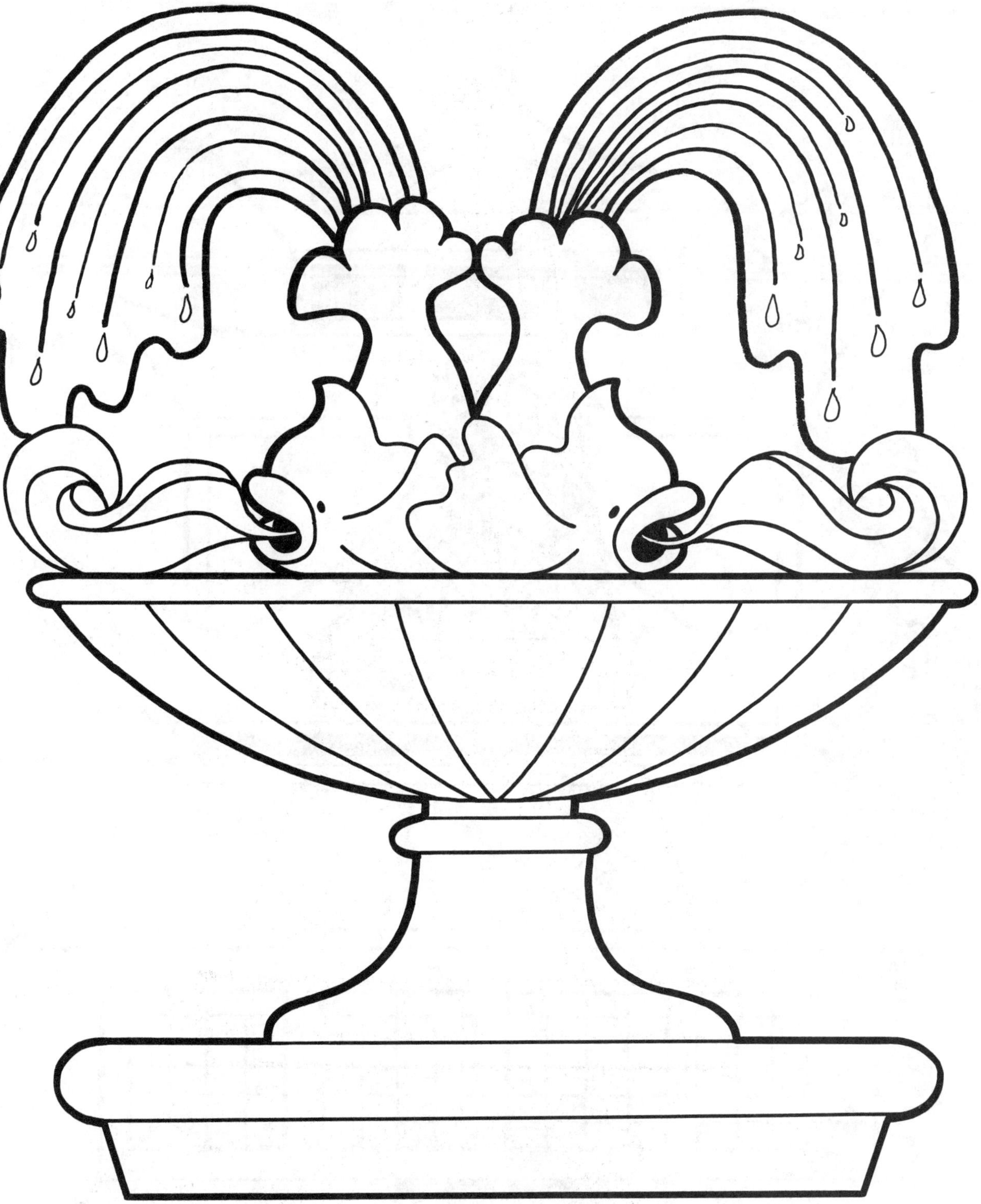

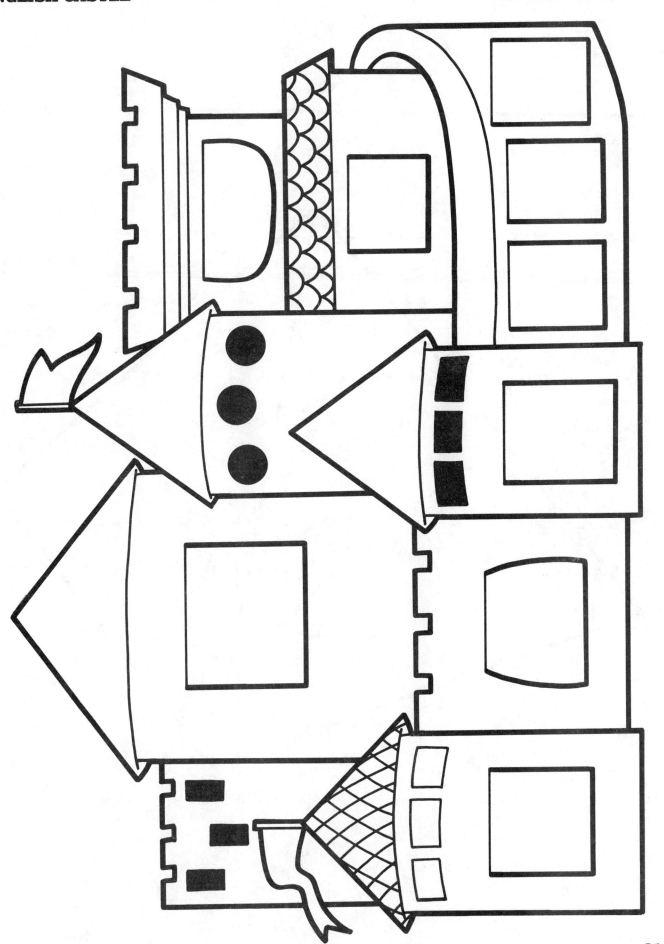

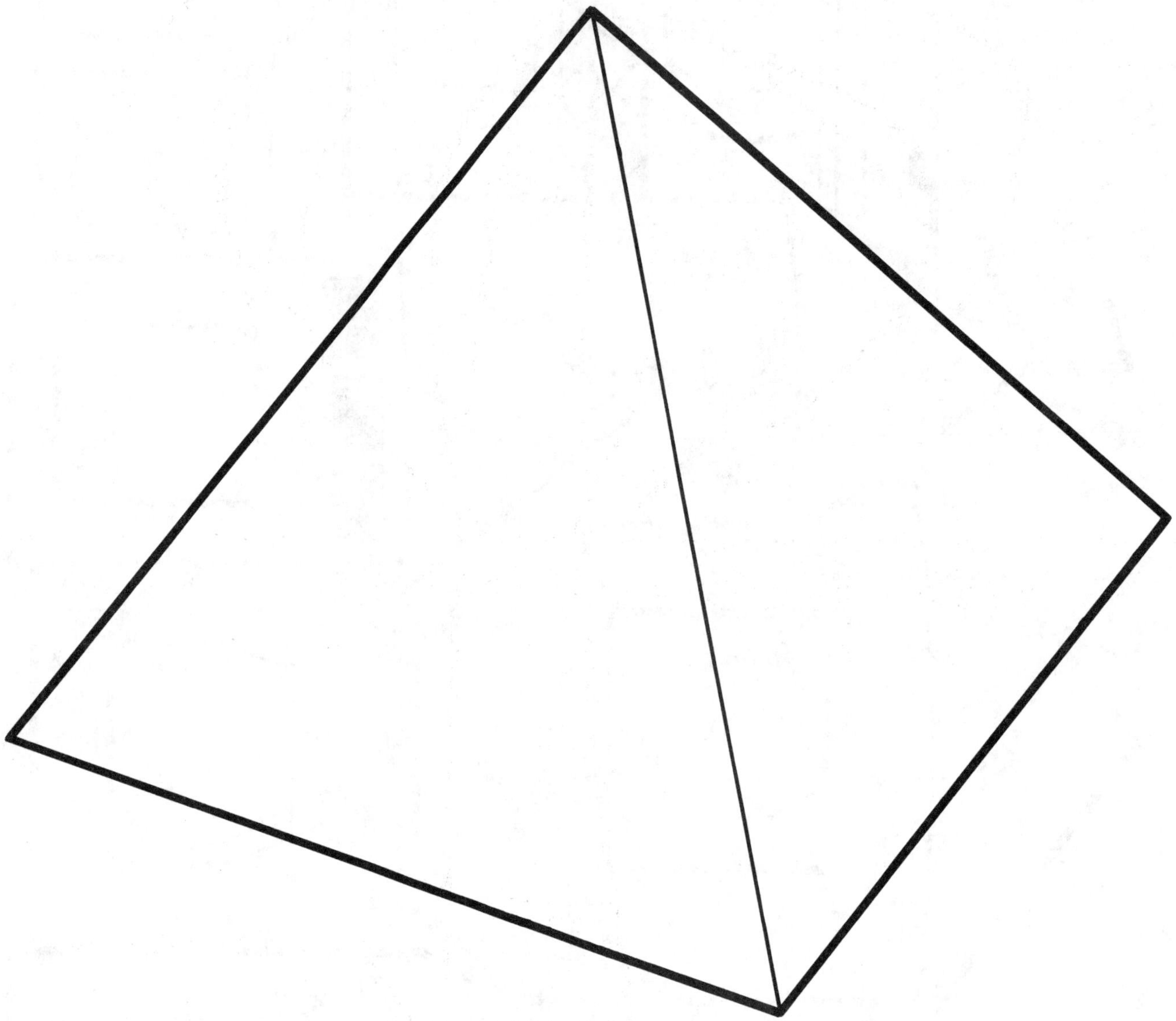

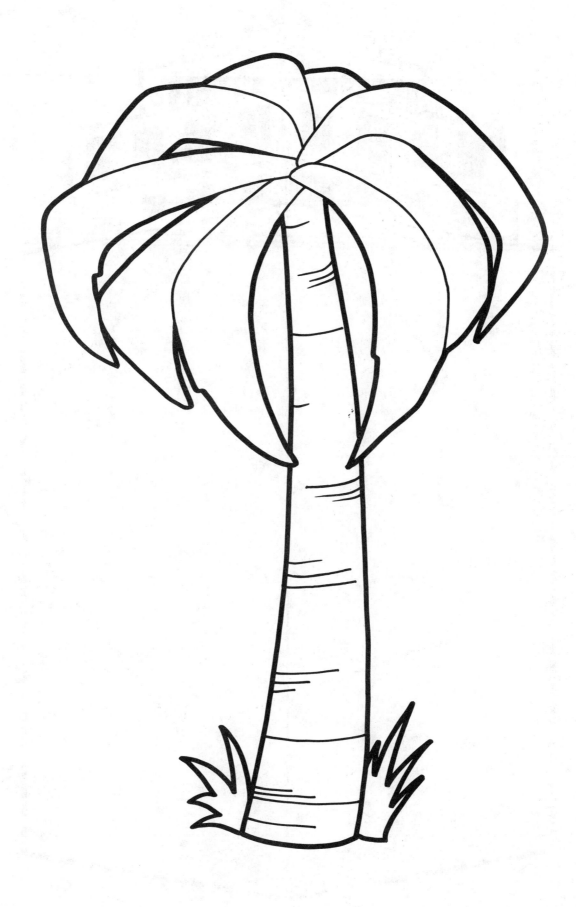

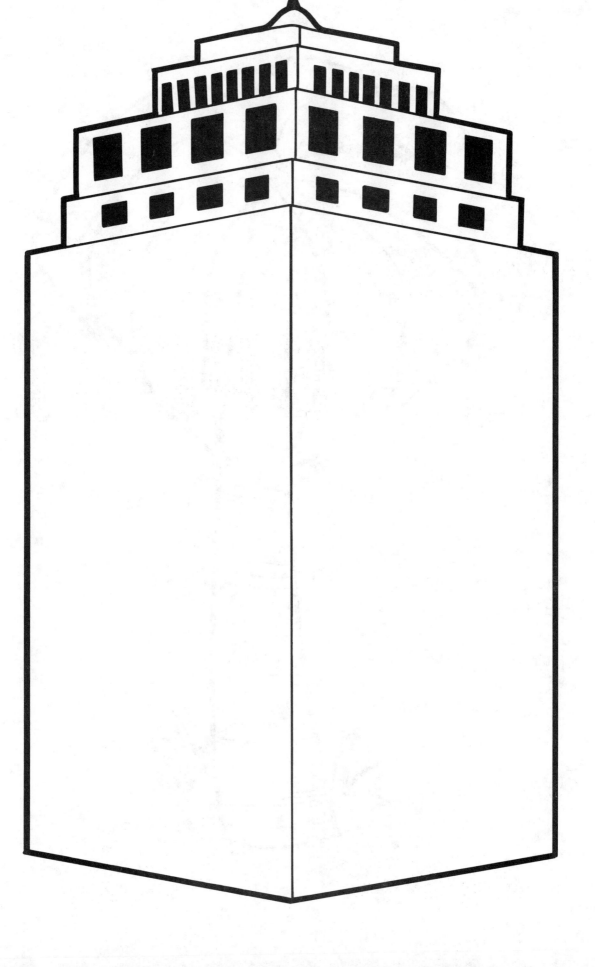

Theme 4:

SPORTS

WHO'S ON FIRST?

QUESTION WORD
BALL CARDS

Bob Porter, a baseball player

a sunny Sunday afternoon

the team won when Bob hit a home run

a play-off game

because both teams had played well

at Rainbow Ball Park

It was a sunny Sunday afternoon at the Rainbow Ball Park. It was near the end of the big play-off game. Bob Porter was at bat. Bob hit a home run and his team won the game. It was a good game because both teams played well.

Who's on First?

OBJECTIVE

The students will use the question words: who, what, where, when, how, and why.

MATERIALS

- Enlargement of the baseball player, page 78
- Construction paper for caption
- Sentence strips
- Tagboard
- Story paper
- 7 pushpins

OTHER CAPTIONS

- *Reporting the Game*
- *Interviewing the Players*
- *Batter Up!*
- *Double, Triple, or Homer?*

PROCEDURE

1. Staple the baseball player to the board.

2. Prepare and staple the caption to the board.

3. On story paper, print a story similar to the one in the illustration. Staple the story to the board.

4. On sentence strips, print phrases that answer the question words. (Use the phrases in the illustration as examples.) Staple the phrases to the board and place a pushpin to the left of each one.

5. Make six tagboard answer cards, designed to resemble baseballs, as shown. Print a different question word on each one. Punch a hole in the top of each.

6. Position a pushpin to hold the baseball cards when not in use.

ACTIVITIES

▶ Have the students read the story and the phrases. Then have them place the correct baseball beside each phrase.

▶ Have the students write the question that each phrase answers. Each question must begin with one of the question words. Example: Who is Bob Porter?

VARIATIONS

● Put the phrases on the board and have the students write stories using the phrases.

● On the sentence strips, print questions about the story. Print the possible answers on the baseballs. Have the students match the answers to the questions.

● Write several paragraphs about the same topic and number each one. Print the main idea of each paragraph on a sentence strip. Print the number of each paragraph on a baseball. Then have the students match the number of the paragraph with its main idea.

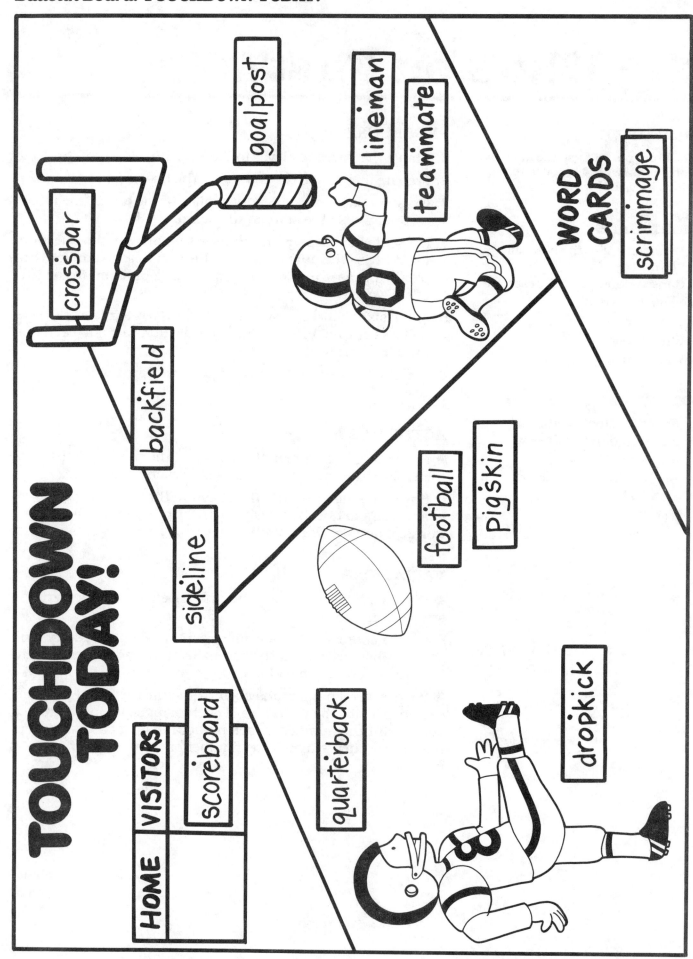

TOUCHDOWN TODAY!

goal post

lineman

teammate

crossbar

backfield

sideline

WORD CARDS

scrimmage

football

Pigskin

dropkick

quarterback

HOME VISITORS

scoreboard

Touchdown Today!

OBJECTIVE

The students will identify compound words.

MATERIALS

- Enlargements of the football kicker, the other football player, and the football, pages 79–80
- Construction paper for caption, goalposts, and scoreboard
- Sentence strips
- 13 pushpins

OTHER CAPTIONS

- *Two-Point Words*
- *Points After Touchdowns*
- *Kickoff*
- *On the Scoreboard*

PROCEDURE

1. Staple the enlargements to the board.
2. Prepare the caption and staple it to the board.
3. Prepare the scoreboard and goalpost as shown and staple them to the board.
4. Print the following compound words and distractors on sentence strips: scoreboard, sideline, backfield, crossbar, goalpost, football, pigskin, dropkick, quarterback, lineman, teammate, helmet, fumble, scrimmage, and referee. Cut the words apart and punch a hole in the top of each.
5. Position a pushpin next to each item on the board named by one of the compound words.
6. Position pushpins to hold the word cards when not in use.

ACTIVITIES

▶ Have the students sort the cards, select the compound words, and hang them on the pushpins.

▶ Have the students identify the two words that form each compound word.

VARIATIONS

● Have the students suggest the compound words for matching.

● Have the students make other compound words using the parts of the compound words displayed on the board. Examples: postcard, chalkboard, boardwalk.

● Have the students arrange the words in alphabetical order.

● Cut apart each compound word between the word parts. Punch a hole in each word part. Display the first half (or the last half) of each word. Then allow the students to match the correct half to make up each compound word.

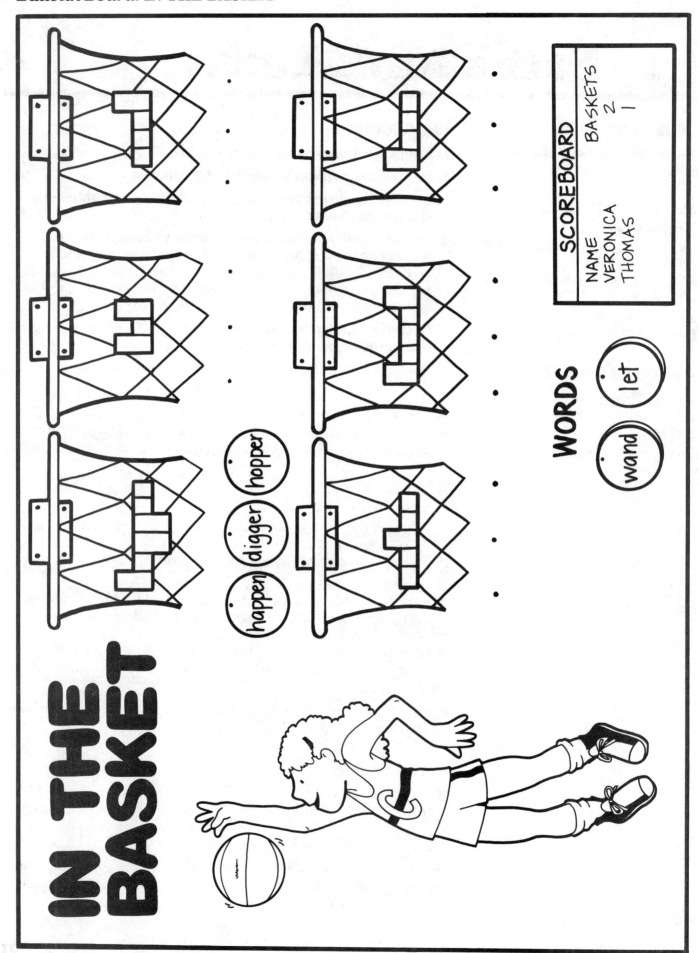

Bulletin Board:

In the Basket

OBJECTIVE

The students will match words with the configurations of the words.

MATERIALS

- Enlargement of the basketball player, page 81
- Construction paper for caption
- Tagboard
- Sentence strips
- 20 pushpins

OTHER CAPTIONS

- *On the Rebound*
- *Dunk 'em!*
- *Hook Shot*
- *Free Throw Time!*

PROCEDURE

1. Staple the basketball player to the board.
2. Prepare and staple the caption to the board.
3. Draw six basketball nets on tagboard, cut them out, and staple them to the board.
4. Draw six different word configurations on tagboard. Cut them out and staple each shape to a net. Two of the suggested configurations are:

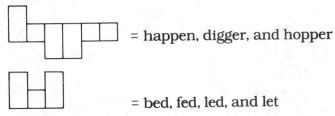

= happen, digger, and hopper

= bed, fed, led, and let

5. Cut out 18 tagboard circles. Place markings on them so they resemble basketballs. Choose three words that conform to each word configuration, and print one word on each basketball. Punch a hole in the top of each.
6. Position three pushpins beneath each net to hold the basketballs.
7. Position remaining pushpins on the board to hold the basketballs when not in use.
8. Optional: Make a scoreboard to record the number of baskets each player earns by making correct matches.

ACTIVITIES

▶ Have the students match the basketball words with the correct configuration blank by hanging the words under the correct nets.

▶ Post the configurations and have the students make the basketball cards from vocabulary lists.

VARIATIONS

● To enrich your students' vocabularies, print "overworked" words on the nets and synonyms on the basketballs for matching. Some word groups to use are big—large, enormous, gigantic—or say—shout, speak, express.

● Review words with multiple meanings, such as set, run, and bank, by placing these words on the nets. Print the meanings on the basketballs for matching.

FROM TEE TO GREEN

From Tee to Green

OBJECTIVE

The students will associate words of common terminal sounds to construct sentences.

MATERIALS

- Enlargement of the golfer, page 82
- Construction paper for caption
- Tagboard in five colors
- 40 pushpins

OTHER CAPTIONS

- *Hole in One*
- *Sand Trap*
- *Bogey, Birdie, or Eagle?*
- *Up to Par*

PROCEDURE

1. Staple the golfer to the board.
2. Prepare the caption and staple it to the board.
3. Cut out five golf hole flags, one from each color. Number them as shown and staple them to the board.
4. Cut out a set of eight golf balls from each color. On each set print words that have the same terminal sound, some articles or determiners, and a verb if needed. A sample set is big, dig, fig, jig, pig, wig, a, can. Punch a hole in the top of each golf ball.
5. Position seven pushpins in horizontal lines from the golfer to each flag.
6. Place a pushpin on the other side of each flag to hold the golf balls when not in use.

ACTIVITIES

▶ Using one set of golf balls at a time, have the students construct a sentence. Show the completed sentence by hanging the chosen golf balls on the row of pushpins leading to the flag of the matching color. You may also wish to accept nonsense sentences that reflect standard syntax.

▶ Display a set of words. Have the students write sentences using the given words.

VARIATIONS

● Supply the terminal sounds but have the students suggest the words to be printed on the golf balls.

● Scramble all the sets of cards and have the students compose sentences.

● Glue a picture on each flag. Glue pictures of objects with the same terminal sound on each set of golf balls. Have the students read the words aloud after matching golf ball pictures to flags. Mix the colors to avoid matching by color.

HEADING THE WORD

safe

WORD CARDS

en

rn

Heading the Word

OBJECTIVE

The students will recognize words with the prefixes **un-**, **re-**, and **dis-**.

MATERIALS

- Enlargement of the soccer kicker, page 83
- Construction paper for caption
- Tagboard for balls
- Sentence strips

OTHER CAPTIONS

- *Dribbling*
- *Go for a Goal*
- *Trapping*
- *Corner Kicking*

PROCEDURE

1. Staple the soccer player to the board.
2. Prepare the caption and staple it to the board.
3. Cut out three circles from tagboard. Draw designs on them so they resemble soccer balls. Staple them to the board with three staples, allowing space to slide the word cards under each ball.
4. Print words with the selected prefixes on the sentence strips and include some distractors. Cut the words apart. Some words to use are unhappy, unsafe, uncurled, uncertain, uneaten, uncover, unpack, unclean, unload, and unripe; return, rebuild, rejoin, rewrite, and renew; and dislike, displease, disappear, dismiss, dishonest, and disfavor. Some distractors are unite, under, uncle, real, ready, read, rent, dish, and distance.
5. Make a pocket to store the word cards when not in use: Cut a piece of tagboard about twice as wide as the cards are tall, then fold it up one third and staple the sides of the folded piece to the board.

ACTIVITIES

▶ Have the students slide each word card under a soccer ball until only the root word shows. The root word may be given orally or in writing. The distractors may be posted separately.

▶ Have the students supply the words for the word cards.

VARIATIONS

● Vary the prefixes or use suffixes.

● Print a root word on each soccer ball. On sentence strips, print prefixes and suffixes that can be used with the root words.

Examples: | re | | ment |

Have the students build words by sliding an affix card under a soccer ball. Discuss the meanings of the new words and/or have the students use them in sentences.

● Print the suffixes that add the meaning of a person who does something (**-er/-or**, **-ist**, **-ress**) on the soccer balls. On the sentence strips, print words that use these suffixes. Have the students sort the words by suffix.

Your Serve!

OBJECTIVE

The students will identify accented syllables.

MATERIALS

- Enlargement of the tennis player, page 84
- Construction paper for caption
- Tagboard
- Butcher paper for tennis net
- Sentence strips
- 20 pushpins

OTHER CAPTIONS

- *Jump the Net*
- *Tennis, Anyone?*
- *Tennis Time*

PROCEDURE

1. Staple the tennis player to the board.
2. Prepare the caption and staple it to the board.
3. Draw a tennis net outline on the butcher paper and staple it to the board.
4. On the sentence strips, print nine two-syllable words from a current vocabulary list. Cut the words apart and staple them to the board.
5. Position a pushpin above each syllable of each word.
6. Cut out 9 circles from the tagboard. Draw tennis ball markings on the circles. Punch a hole at the top of each one.
7. Position a pushpin on the board to hold the tennis balls when not in use.

ACTIVITIES

▶ Have the students pronounce each word and identify the accented syllable by hanging a tennis ball above it.

▶ Have the students list all the words which are accented on the first syllable and all those which are accented on the second.

▶ Have the students copy the words and show the syllable breaks.

VARIATIONS

● Use words of three or more syllables.

● Display words whose accented syllables change when a suffix is added. Examples: family and familiar, exhibit and exhibition. Have the students find the accent changes.

● Display pairs of words whose meanings and pronunciations change as the accents change. Some pairs are re cord' and rec'ord, de sert' and des'ert, sub ject' and sub'ject, con tract' and con'tract, mi nute' and min'ute. Write one meaning on each tennis ball and challenge the students to make the matches.

LINEMAN/TEAMMATE

FOOTBALL

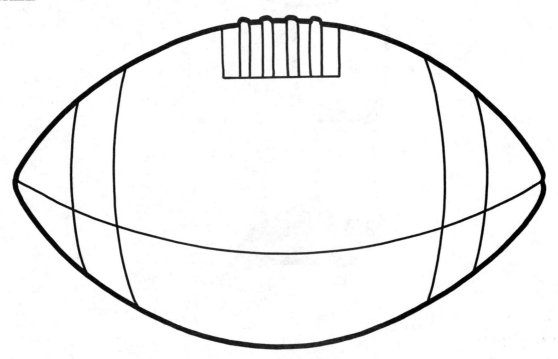

Theme 5:

SPACE AGE

SAIL TO THE STARS?

PARAGRAPH NUMBER CARDS

5

1

3

1. This star has all white points. There is a dark ring in the middle of the star. Inside the ring is a big white spot.

2. There is a white ring inside this star. It circles a big dark spot in the middle. This star has all white points.

3. Three dark points are together on this star. The two white points blend with open space in the middle of the star. There is no other design on this star.

4. This star has three white points and two dark points. One dark point faces up while the other faces down. There's a circle in the middle.

5. There are no dark areas on this star. It has two circles in the center. A little circle is inside the big circle.

Sail to the Stars?

OBJECTIVE

The students will demonstrate reading comprehension.

MATERIALS

- Enlargement of the rocket ship, page 98
- Construction paper
- Tagboard
- 10 pushpins

OTHER CAPTIONS

- *Seeing Stars*
- *Be a Star*
- *Reach for the Stars*

PROCEDURE

1. Staple the rocket ship to the board.
2. Prepare the caption and staple it to the board.
3. Cut eight stars from construction paper. Put a unique design on each star. (More subtle design differences will require higher levels of comprehension.) Staple the stars to the board. Position a pushpin next to each star.
4. Compose five short paragraphs, each describing a different star. Print each paragraph on a piece of construction paper. Number the paragraphs 1–5 and staple them to the board.
5. Make answer cards by cutting 2″ by 3″ rectangles from tagboard and numbering them 1–5. Punch a hole in the top of each card.
6. Position a pushpin on the board to hold the answer cards when not in use.

ACTIVITIES

▶ Have the students study the stars and read the paragraphs. Then ask them to match each star to its paragraph by hanging the number of the paragraph beside the correct star.

▶ Have the students write paragraphs describing the three remaining stars.

VARIATIONS

● Have the students write the paragraphs that describe each star and use their paragraphs for oral reading.

● On sentence strips, print sentences with key words omitted. Print the missing words on the stars. Use some distractors, too!

● Print statements to place on the rocket ship. Use statements such as "Name three parts of a hand," "Name three parts of a face," and "Name three parts of a foot." On the stars, print words that satisfy the rocket statement requests. Have the students match the star words to the rocket statements.

BLAST OFF!

CARD BANK

alien · both · astronaut

I travel in a spaceship.

I will learn to speak Earth languages.

I want to make friends.

I have only three fingers.

I am not human.

I was born on the planet Earth.

I have traveled in space.

I was not born on the planet Earth.

I wear a spacesuit.

I am an explorer.

astronaut

Blast Off!

OBJECTIVE

The students will draw conclusions from given facts.

MATERIALS

- Enlargements of the rocket ship, alien, and astronaut, pages 98–100
- Construction paper for caption
- Tagboard
- Sentence strips
- 13 pushpins

OTHER CAPTIONS

- *Roaring into Space*
- *In Orbit*
- *One or Many*

PROCEDURE

1. Staple the rocket ship, the alien, and the astronaut to the board as shown.
2. Prepare the caption and staple it to the board.
3. Print the statements shown in the illustration on the sentence strips. Staple them to the board and position a push-pin to the left of each strip.
4. Cut 15 tagboard circles. Print "alien" on five circles, "astronaut" on five circles, and "both" on five circles. Punch a hole in the top of each circle.
5. Position three pushpins on the board to hold the answer circles when not in use.

ACTIVITIES

▶ Have the students read each statement, choose the correct answer circles, and hang them in place.

▶ Have the students rewrite the sentences replacing "I" with "The alien," "The astronaut," or "Both."

VARIATIONS

● Write five yes and five no statements on the sentence strips. Example: An astronaut flies in a spaceship. Print five "yes" and five "no" circle cards. Have the students match the circle card answers to the questions.

● On the sentence strips, write sentences which contain words that can be contracted. Example: The alien cannot swim. Write the contractions on the answer circles for matching.

● On sentence strips, print sentences that tell a story. Jumble the strips and staple them to the board. Number an answer circle for each strip. Have the students place the appropriate answer circles beside the sentences to show the correct numerical order.

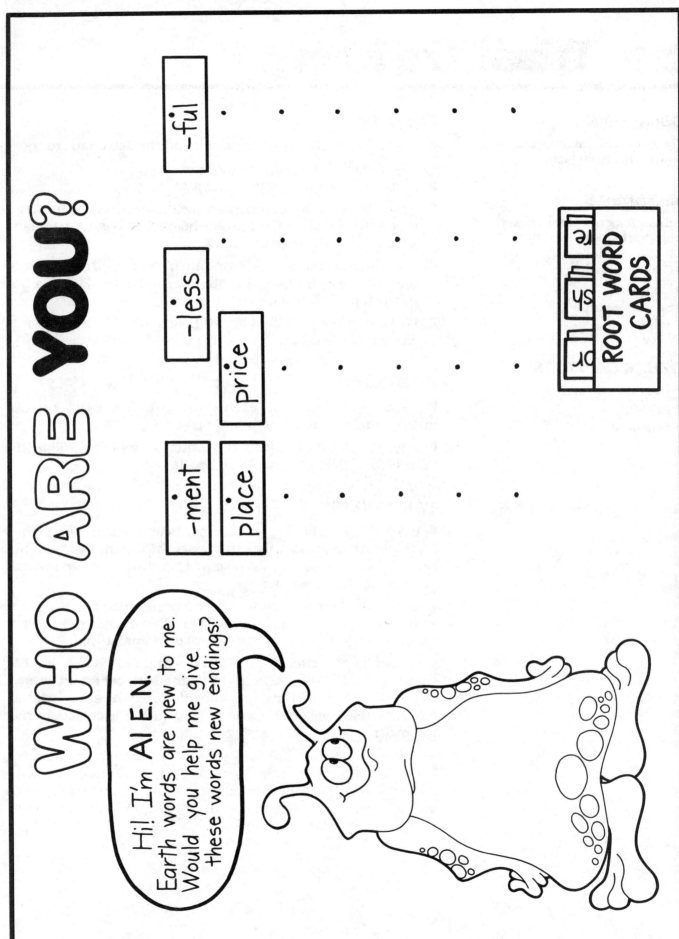

Who Are You?

OBJECTIVE

The students will use the suffixes **-ment**, **-less**, and **-ful**.

MATERIALS

- Enlargement of the alien, page 99
- Construction paper for caption
- Tagboard
- 24 pushpins

OTHER CAPTIONS

- *Al E. N. Learns English*
- *Teach Al E. N.*
- *What Do You Mean?*

PROCEDURE

1. Staple the alien to the board.
2. Prepare the caption and staple it to the board.
3. Cut a speech balloon from tagboard and print this message on it: "Hi, I'm Al E. N. Earth words are new to me. Would you help me give these words new endings?" Staple the speech balloon to the board.
4. Cut three tagboard cards and print one of these suffixes on each card: **-ment**, **-less**, and **-ful**. Staple the cards to the board. Position a column of six pushpins under **-ment** and under **-ful**. Position two columns of six pushpins under **-less**.
5. On tagboard cards, print words that can use the given suffixes. Print duplicates of the words that can use two of the given suffixes. Suggested word list: enjoy, govern, place, treat, base, develop, life, friend, change, bottom, help, thank, play, cheer, care, fruit, power. Punch a hole in the top of each word card.
6. Make a pocket to hold the word cards by folding a piece of tagboard up one third and stapling it on either side to the board. Position the pocket near one of the alien's hands.

ACTIVITIES

▶ Have the students sort the cards into the correct suffix categories and hang the cards in place.

▶ Have the students write sentences using the words with suffixes.

VARIATIONS

● Have the students supply the words from current reading vocabularies.

● Change the suffix categories or use prefixes instead of suffixes.

● Use the meanings of the affixes as categories. Examples: not, full of, in the past. On word cards, print complete words that contain the chosen affix meanings. Examples: unhappy, joyous, jumped. Have the students sort the word cards into categories defined by the affix meanings.

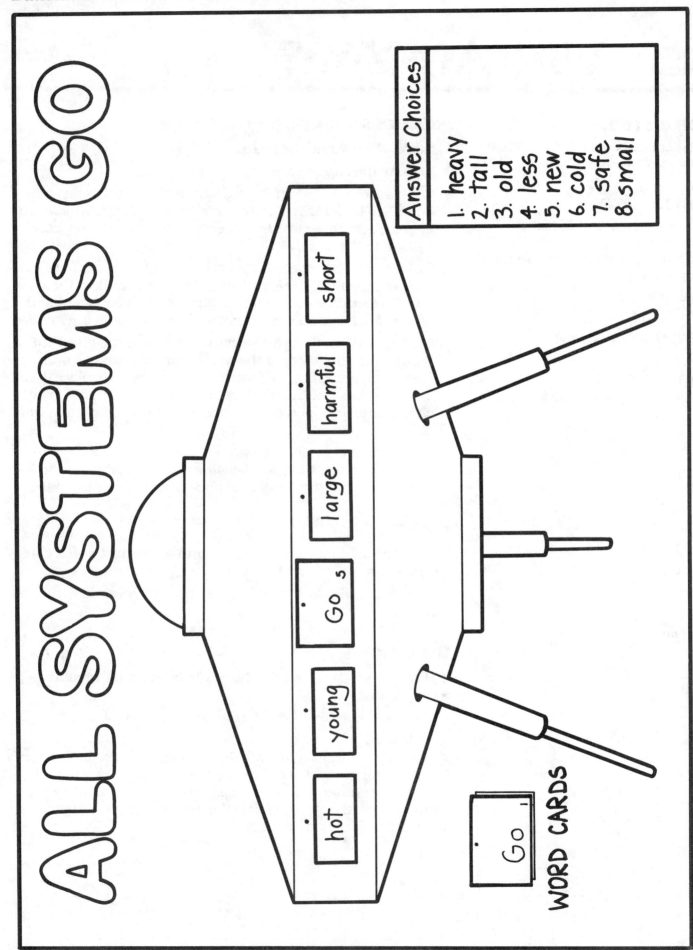

All Systems Go

OBJECTIVE

The students will find antonyms for the given words.

MATERIALS

- Enlargement of the lunar module, page 101
- Construction paper for caption and answer choice card
- Red and green tagboard
- 7 pushpins

OTHER CAPTIONS

- *Exploring*
- *Strange Territory*
- *Looking at _____ (Use name of unit.)*

PROCEDURE

1. Staple the lunar module to the board.
2. Prepare the caption and staple it to the board.
3. Cut six red tagboard rectangles sized to match the windows in the lunar module. Choose six vocabulary words; print one on each red card, and staple one card in each window of the lunar module. Position a pushpin above each word card.
4. Make the answer choice card: On a piece of construction paper, print one antonym for each of the six vocabulary words as well as two distractors. Number the choices 1–8. Staple the answer choice card to the board.
5. Cut six green rectangles a little taller than the red rectangles. Print "Go" on each card. Number the "Go" cards 1–6. Punch a hole in the top of each card.
6. Position a pushpin on the board to hold the "Go" cards when not in use.

ACTIVITIES

▶ Have the students read a word on the lunar module, find its correct antonym on the answer choice card, and place the "Go" card with the number of the correct answer over the word on the window. When all the windows are covered, "All systems are **Go!**"

▶ Have the students write sentences using the window words and their antonyms.

VARIATIONS

● Have the students suggest the words and/or the antonyms.

● Use synonyms instead of antonyms.

● Print a riddle on each window card and list the answers on the answer choice card.

● Print an idiom on each window card and the meanings on the answer choice card.

● Print questions from your current social studies unit on the window cards and the answers on the answer choice card.

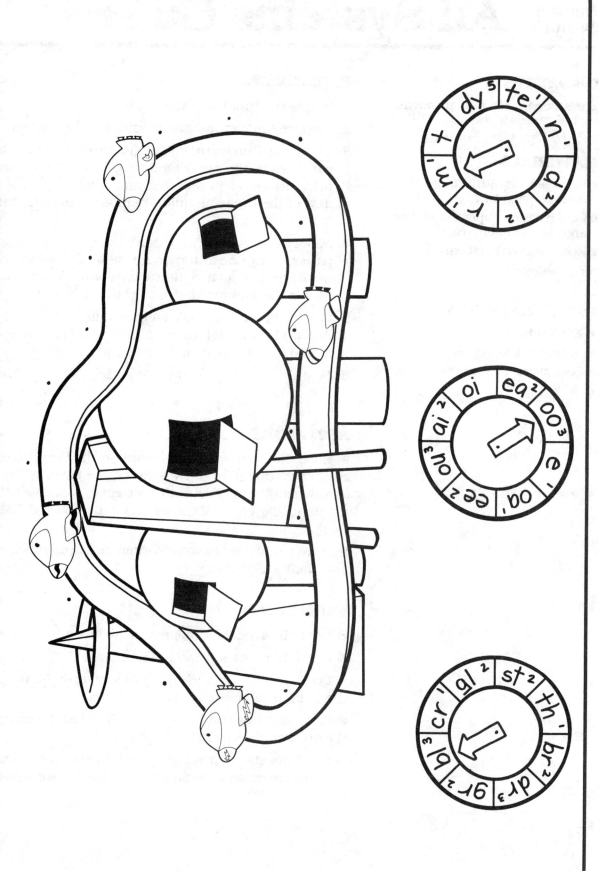

Bulletin Board:

Future City Freeway

OBJECTIVE

The students will make words using the given letters.

MATERIALS

- Enlargement of the future city, page 102
- Construction paper for caption
- Space cars, page 103
- Tagboard
- Three brads
- 35–40 pushpins

OTHER CAPTIONS

- *Dialing for Words*
- *Find That Car!*
- *Words of the Future*

PROCEDURE

1. Staple the enlarged future city to the board.
2. Prepare the caption and staple it to the board.
3. Make a tagboard space car for each student. (Enlarge or reduce the car size to suit the size of the freeway.) Punch a hole in the top of each car.
4. Place pushpins along the freeway, as shown.
5. Prepare three tagboard dials as shown in the illustration. The first dial contains initial consonant blends, the second dial contains vowel digraphs, and the third dial contains terminal sounds. Assign point values at random to each sound wedge.
6. Staple the dials to the board, making sure the arrows are balanced and can spin freely. (Dials may need to be placed on a flat surface near bulletin board.)

ACTIVITIES

▶ Each player will need paper, pencil, and a space car. Set a time limit for the game. Have the players take turns spinning all three arrows to make real words. The player adds together the number of points from each portion of the constructed word and moves his or her car forward that many spaces after recording the word on paper. The player in the lead when time is up is the winner.

▶ Let the students make real or nonsense words; they can print their favorite words on the space cars and hang the cars on the freeway.

VARIATIONS

● Have the students design a car of the future, sized to fit the freeway, and name it using the given sounds. Then have the students think of other words that use these sounds. Have them print the new words on small circles and staple the circles to the board as exhaust coming from the appropriate vehicle.

● Use only one dial. Print words on the space cars that use the sounds on the dial. Hang up the cars. Have the students spin the arrow and find the car with the word containing that sound.

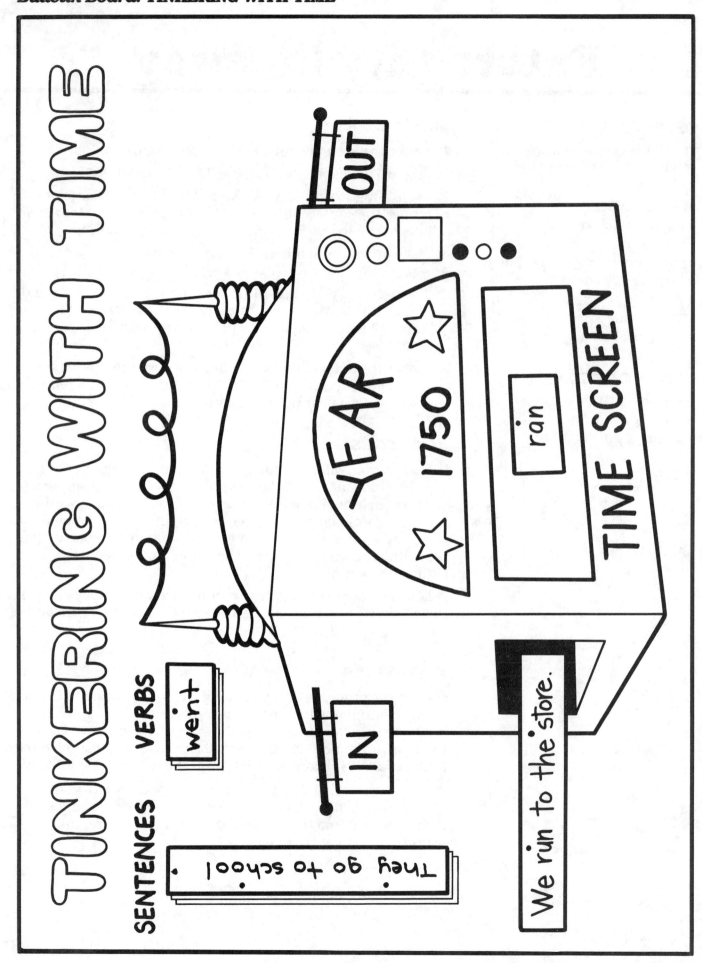

Tinkering with Time

OBJECTIVE

The students will identify the past tense forms of regular and irregular verbs.

MATERIALS

- Enlargement of the time machine, page 104
- Construction paper for caption
- Sentence strips
- 5 pushpins

OTHER CAPTIONS

- *Word Time*
- *Eavesdropping on Time*
- *Tinker Today, Will Tinker Tomorrow*

PROCEDURE

1. Staple the time machine to the board.
2. Prepare the caption and staple it to the board.
3. On the sentence strips, print short sentences using different present tense verbs. Punch two holes in the top of each strip. Punch one hole in the short edge so the strips can be stored when not in use.
4. Print the matching past tense verb forms and some distractors on sentence strips and cut them apart. Punch a hole in the top of each.
5. Position two pushpins under the "In" sign of the time machine to hold the displayed present tense sentence strip.
6. Position a pushpin in the time screen of the time machine to hold the matching past tense card.
7. Position pushpins on the board to hold the strips and past tense cards when not in use.

ACTIVITIES

▶ Have the students hang a sentence above the "In" door. Then have the students make the machine "go backward in time" by finding the correct past tense verb and hanging it on the time screen.

▶ Have the students rewrite each sentence in the past tense.

VARIATIONS

● Use present tense verbs instead of sentences. Choose verbs that require doubling the final consonant and/or changing the **-y** to **-i** before adding **-ed**. Write the correct past tense forms on the time screen cards.

● Print a question mark on one time screen card and an exclamation point on another. Have the students rewrite the statements as questions or exclamations.

● Use present or past tense verbs in the sentences. Have the students find the correct form of the future tense.

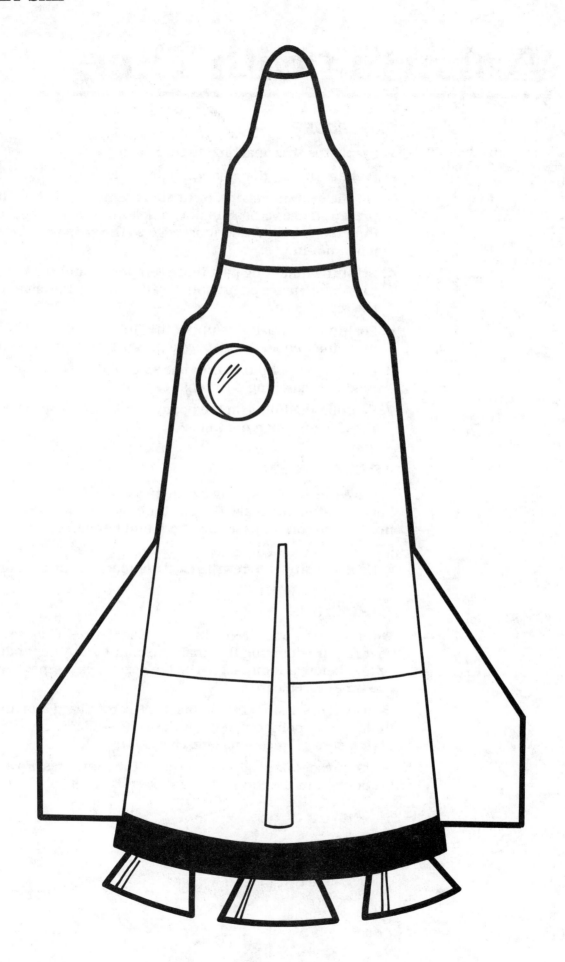

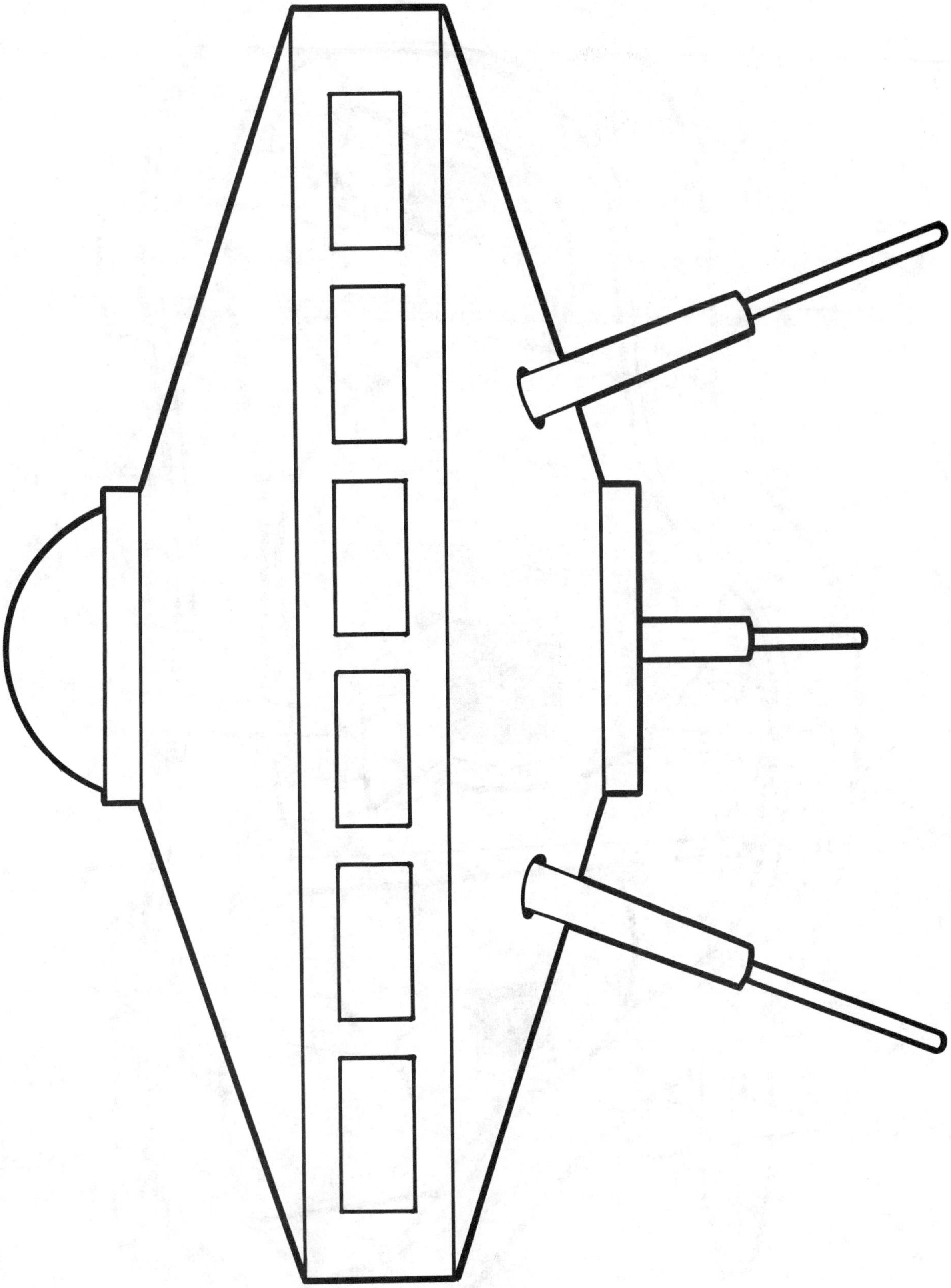

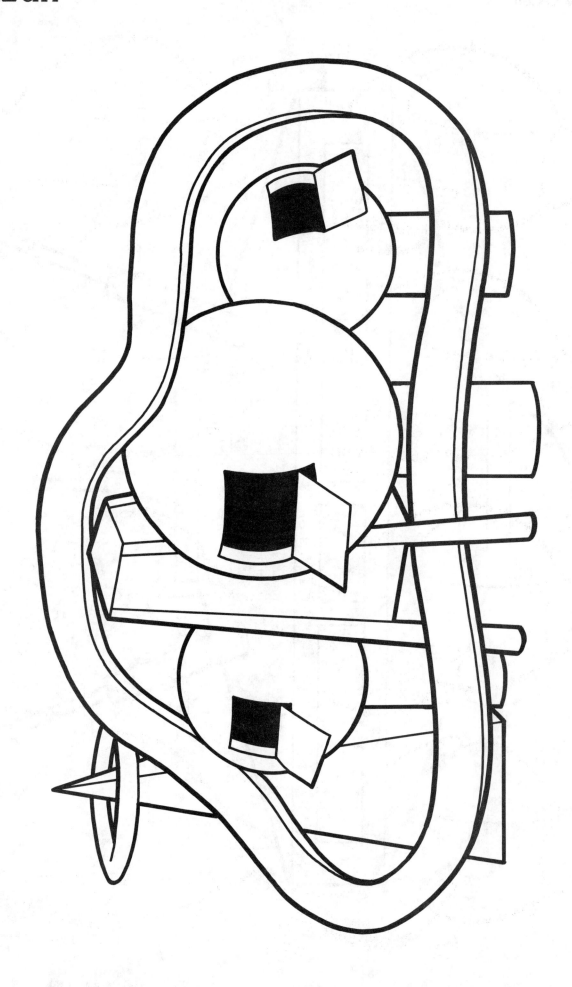

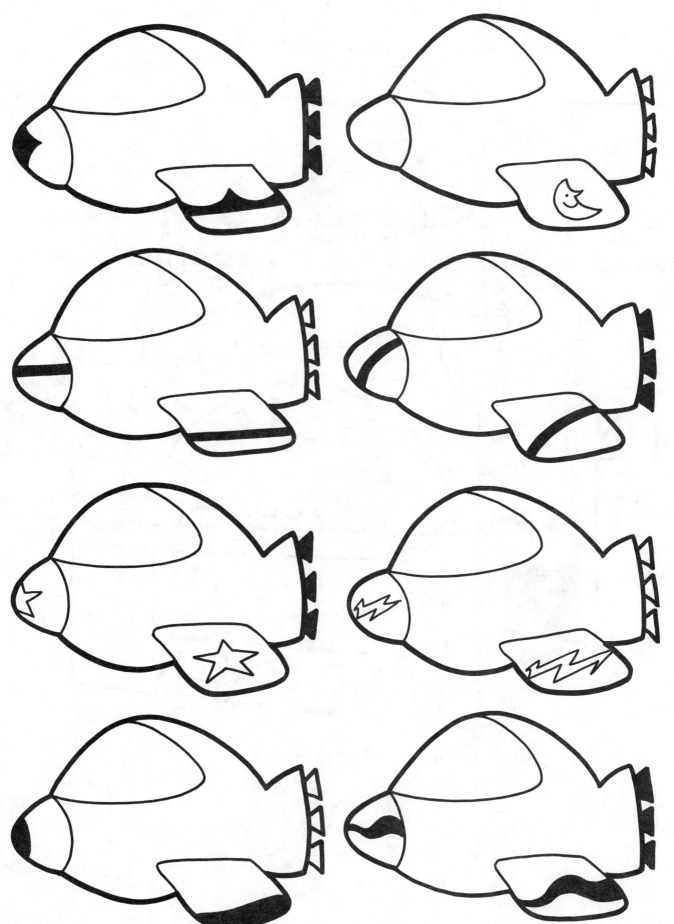

Theme 6:

THE HOLIDAYS

CALENDAR TIME

SEPTEMBER

Sunday	Monday	Tuesday	Wednesday	Thursday	Friday	Saturday
		1	2	3	4	5
6	7	8	9	10		12
13	14		16	17	18	19
20	21	22	23		25	26
27	28	29	30			

Calendar Time

OBJECTIVE

The students will reinforce their calendar reference skills.

MATERIALS

- Enlargement of the calendar grid, page 118
- Enlargement of the month banner and patterns for special day labels, page 119
- Construction paper for caption
- Washable felt-tipped marker
- Clear Con-Tact® vinyl or laminating supplies

OTHER CAPTIONS

- *Day by Day*
- *Time Flies*
- *Yesterday, Today, and Tomorrow*

PROCEDURE

1. Laminate the calendar grid or cover it with clear Con-Tact® vinyl. Staple it to the board.
2. Prepare the caption and staple it to the board.
3. On the first school day of each month, preview the special happenings for that month. You may wish to do this on a weekly basis, too.
4. Number the days of the month with the marker.
5. Prepare the month banner and staple it above the calendar grid.
6. Prepare the special day labels you will need for the month. Cut out and color each label. Your students wil enjoy helping you!
7. Use pushpins to attach the special day labels to the calendar.
8. At the end of each month, wipe off the numbers and repeat steps 3–7.

ACTIVITIES

▶ Use the calendar to motivate your students to learn the days of the week and the months in order.

▶ Familiarize your students with common expressions that describe calendar time; for example, "A week from Tuesday" and "The day before yesterday."

▶ Have the students make appropriate illustrations of special events and display their pictures around the calendar.

VARIATIONS

● Reproduce a small calendar for each student to personalize and refer to as needed.

● Give a student the daily or weekly responsibility of presenting the date to the group. Designate the responsibility on the calendar.

● Have a student design the banner for the month.

● Have your students practice writing abbreviations for the days of the week and the months.

A large pumpkin grew in the garden.

The pumpkin said, "I'm glad it's Halloween."

The pumpkin was hoping to become a giant jack-o-lantern.

On Halloween, children go trick-or-treating.

Goblins roam around on Halloween night.

The moon is bright and full.

The night seems spooky.

A witch flies across the moon on a broom.

WHICH NEEDS A WITCH?

Who needs me?

Which Needs a Witch?

OBJECTIVE

The students will identify statements of fantasy.

MATERIALS

- Enlargement of the Halloween witch, page 120
- Construction paper for caption, speech balloon, and broom heads
- Tagboard for witch's hats
- Sentence strips
- 9 pushpins

OTHER CAPTIONS

- *Witch's Spell*
- *Clean Sweep*
- *Bewitched*
- *Word Witchery*

PROCEDURE

1. Staple the witch to the board.
2. Prepare the caption and staple it to the board.
3. Print statements on the sentence strips. Write some realistic statements and some examples of fantasy. Staple the strips (resembling broomsticks) to the board.
4. Cut out eight broom heads. Staple them to the board at the ends of the broomstick sentence strips.
5. Cut eight witch's hats from tagboard. Punch a hole in the top of each hat.
6. Position a pushpin beside each broom.
7. Position a pushpin on the board to hold the hats when not in use.

ACTIVITIES

▶ Ask a student to read a statement and decide if it is realistic or if it shows fantasy. If the statement would need "a witch to cast a spell to make it happen" (that is, if it shows fantasy), have the student hang a witch's hat beside the statement. Go through all of the statements. Follow up the activity with a discussion of realism and fantasy.

▶ Have the students "cast spells" on the realistic sentences by rewriting them to show fantasy.

VARIATIONS

● Post the weekly spelling words on the broom handles.

● On sentence strips, print some sentences containing homophones and some sentences without homophones. Have the students hang the hats next to the brooms with homophones. Example: "This is the way to weigh the pumpkin."

● Use the board to display Halloween words suggested by the students.

WHAT IS PLYMOUTH?

WORDS WITH MANY MEANINGS

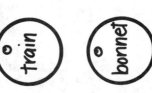

horn

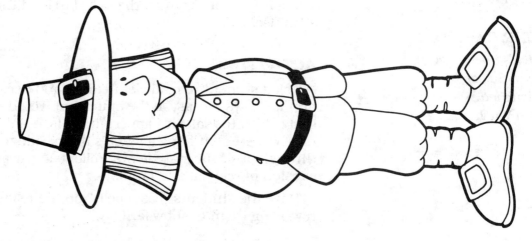

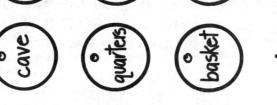

board
bat
train
bonnet

cave
quarters
basket

wick
tracks
hide
cast

What Is Plymouth?

OBJECTIVE

The students will identify words with multiple meanings.

MATERIALS

- Enlargement of the Pilgrim, page 121
- Construction paper for caption and subcaption
- Tagboard
- 24 pushpins

OTHER CAPTIONS

- *Thanks in Many Ways*
- *Say What You Mean*
- *Feasting*
- *What's for Dinner?*

PROCEDURE

1. Staple the Pilgrim to the board.
2. Prepare the caption and subcaption and staple them to the board.
3. Cut 12 circles from tagboard. On some circles, print words with multiple meanings. On the rest of the circles, print words that have single meanings. Punch a hole in the top of each circle.
4. Position 12 pushpins to the left of the Pilgrim and suspend the word circles as shown.
5. Position 12 pushpins to the right of the Pilgrim.

ACTIVITIES

▶ Have the students sort the words and hang the ones with multiple meanings under the subcaption. Encourage your students to use dictionaries if they're unsure of a word's meanings.

▶ Have the students suggest the words for the word circles. Have them use the words in sentences.

▶ Discuss the word "Plymouth." It refers to a rock, a city, and a type of car!

VARIATIONS

● To show that Thanksgiving has many meanings, have the students write sentences about Thanksgiving and post them on the board.

● Read the story of the first Thanksgiving. Then have the students retell the story as you record it. Write their version on tagboard and post it on the board. Then have the students find words with multiple meanings in their story. Some words may be grain, corn, squash, meal, and fall.

● Print Thanksgiving foods on sentence strips and cut the words apart. Make categories, such as fruits, vegetables, meats, and desserts, and have the students sort the words into the correct categories.

Which One Is Mine?

OBJECTIVE

The students will identify the meanings of given homophones.

MATERIALS

- Enlargement of Santa Claus, page 122
- Construction paper for caption, speech balloon, and gifts
- Tagboard
- 11 pushpins

OTHER CAPTIONS

- *Loading Santa's Bag*
- *Heavy, Heavy Over Your Head*
- *Christmas Concentration*

PROCEDURE

1. Staple Santa to the board.
2. Prepare the caption and staple it to the board.
3. Prepare Santa's speech balloon and staple it to the board as shown.
4. Cut out 10 rectangular tagboard "gifts," decorated with bows and ribbons as shown. Print a pair of homophone meanings on them, one on each half. Staple the gifts to the board and position a pushpin on each gift.
5. Cut 15 rectangular name tags from tagboard. Print the pairs of homophones that match the gift meanings on 10 tags. On the remaining tags, switch the order of some of the homophones. Some homophones to use are ate/eight, cents/sense, threw/through, whole/hole, soar/sore, here/hear, two/too, heir/air, grown/groan, some/sum.
6. Position a pushpin to hold the name tags when not in use.

ACTIVITIES

▶ Have the students read the meanings on both halves of each package, sort the name tags, select those that match the meanings in proper order, and hang the tags over the correct packages.

▶ Have the students make the homophone name tags match the meanings on the packages.

▶ Have the students use the homophones in sentences.

VARIATIONS

● Glue pictures on each gift and cut a slit in Santa's bag large enough to slide a gift through. Have the students study the board, and then close their eyes while one person removes a gift and slips it in the bag. Challenge the students to recall the gift that was removed.

● Lead the group in a game of Twenty Questions. Glue a picture on each gift. Turn the gifts face down. Have the students ask "yes" or "no" questions to determine what each gift is. Reveal the picture of each gift as it is guessed.

Straight to Your Heart

OBJECTIVE

The students will identify silent consonants.

MATERIALS

- Enlargement of the cupid, page 123
- Construction paper for caption
- Tagboard
- 13 pushpins

OTHER CAPTIONS

- *Silent Hearts*
- *Valentine Kit*
- *Our Favorites*

PROCEDURE

1. Staple the enlargement of the cupid to the board.
2. Prepare the caption and staple it to the board.
3. Cut out 12 hearts from tagboard. Print a word that begins with a silent consonant on 10 of the hearts. Print words that do not begin with a silent consonant on the other two hearts. Staple the hearts to the board and position a pushpin above each one.
4. Cut out 12 arrows from tagboard. Punch a hole in the feathered end of each arrow.
5. Position a pushpin on the board to hold the arrows when not in use.

ACTIVITIES

▶ Have the students read the words and place arrows over the hearts whose words begin with silent consonants.

▶ Have the students suggest words that begin with silent consonants. Write them on the hearts for displaying on the board.

VARIATIONS

● Use words that have silent medial or terminal consonants. Examples: whistle, wrestle, thumb, or lamb. You could also use words with silent vowels: train, make, or bean.

● Hang pictures of items that have silent letters when spelled out. Have the students spell the words.

● Use the board as a valentine construction center. Post simple instructions on the board for making a valentine. Supply the needed materials.

● Have the students bring in pictures of things (objects, hobbies, pets, places, etc.) they especially like. Post the pictures on the hearts, and have the students explain their choices orally or in writing.

EGGS-ACTLY RIGHT!

Robin Rabbit was busy bringing springtime to town. She delivered many eggs. Her first stop was at the yellow house with two chimneys. Then she stopped at a house with two chimneys and two doors. Next she went to a wide house with two doors and two windows. Her next stop was at a red house with one long window. The fifth house she visited had a window above the door and a chimney on the left side. The last house she stopped at has three windows and a purple chimney.

EGG CARDS

Eggs-actly Right!

OBJECTIVE

The students will arrange the given events in chronological order (and demonstrate reading comprehension).

MATERIALS

- Enlargement of Robin Rabbit, page 124
- Construction paper for caption
- Tagboard
- Story paper
- 7 pushpins

OTHER CAPTIONS

- *Hopalong Bunny*
- *Bunny's Helper*
- *Egg Roll*

PROCEDURE

1. Staple the rabbit to the board.
2. Prepare the caption and staple it to the board.
3. Use the tagboard to make six or more houses. Decorate them so that each house is distinctly different. Staple the houses to the board.
4. Position a pushpin in the bottom left corner of each house.
5. Cut out six eggs from tagboard and number them 1–6. Punch a hole in the top of each egg.
6. Position a pushpin on the board to hold the eggs when not in use.
7. Write a story on the story paper detailing a sequence of events. For example: "Robin Rabbit was busy bringing springtime to town. She delivered many eggs. Her first stop was at the yellow house with two doors. Then she stopped at a house with one chimney, and . . . " The details must correspond with the house decorations. Staple the story to the board.

ACTIVITIES

▶ Have the students read the story and then hang the numbered eggs by the houses in the order of Robin's stops.

▶ Have the students decorate and number the eggs. They could also write their own stories about Robin.

VARIATIONS

● Rewrite the story so that Robin must deliver certain eggs to specific houses. The students must place the correct eggs beside the correct houses.

● Place the rabbit in the middle of the board with houses on both sides. Label the board halves "Right" and "Left." (Labels should correspond to the viewer—not the rabbit.) Give oral directions (using the words "right" and "left") for the students to "deliver" the eggs.

CALENDAR GRID

Sunday	Monday	Tuesday	Wednesday	Thursday	Friday	Saturday

SPECIAL DAY LABELS FOR CALENDAR

MONTH BANNER

RED-LETTER DAYS

PATRIOTIC DAYS

BIRTHDAYS

PILGRIM

SANTA'S BAG